THE ROYAL COMMISSION ON CRIMINAL JUSTICE

Preparing Records of Taped Interview
by **John Baldwin**

The Role of Legal Representatives at the Police Station
by **John Baldwin**

Supervision of Police Investigation in Serious Criminal Cases
by **John Baldwin** and **Timothy Moloney**

London: HMSO

© Crown copyright 1992
Applications for reproduction should be made for HMSO
First published 1992

ISBN 0 11 341050 6

Any views expressed in this report are those of the author(s) and do not necessarily reflect the views of the Royal Commission

Acknowledgements

Conducting research as part of the Royal Commission's programme has proved a rewarding, if exacting, undertaking. While it has offered many new and exciting opportunities to tackle issues that have scarcely been researched in the past, the very tight deadlines, to which all the Commission's researchers have been subject, have inevitably limited the scope of the enquiries that could be carried out.

The three studies in this volume have, however, been greatly facilitated by the high level of cooperation received in all quarters. I am extremely grateful to the Royal Commission on Criminal Justice for funding the studies and particularly to Julie Vennard of its Secretariat, who has offered a great deal of advice and help over the past year.

I am also indebted to the police forces which participated in the three projects. While the West Midlands, Metropolitan and West Mercia Forces have shouldered the main burden, several others, particularly the Hampshire, Northamptonshire and Leicestershire Forces offered willing assistance at different stages. When I found that I needed research materials at short notice, every effort was made to meet my requests, despite the difficulties that this inevitably created for the individuals concerned. Officers of all ranks within those forces did much to encourage and facilitate my work, as did the Crown Prosecutors and the firms of solicitors I contacted.

Mr Tony Payne of the Policy and Communications Group of the Crown Prosecution Service and Mr John Woodcock of F2 Division of the Home Office gave me much useful assistance, and their willingness to help was much appreciated. My colleague, Dr Richard Young, also read drafts of each of the three studies and offered many valuable insights and criticisms of them.

I should stress that, in thanking these people for their generous assistance in carrying out the studies, none is responsible for the views expressed in these reports. The views are mine alone and are not to be taken as those of the police service, the Royal Commission or any other body.

Professor John Baldwin
Institute of Judicial Administration
University of Birmingham   August 1992

PREPARING THE RECORD OF TAPED INTERVIEW

JOHN BALDWIN

Background to the study

Few people dispute the desirability of recording police officers' interviews with suspects. The fears that were voiced in the 1970s about the consequence of using tape recorders – that they would lead to endless accusations of tampering and to suspects faking beatings, for example – have simply not materialised.[1] Once the police service set its mind to it, the transition to tape recording was achieved speedily and painlessly, and it is difficult now to muster a single genuine argument against its use.[2] It is a rarity to encounter innovation within the criminal justice system that is welcomed in all quarters, and it is perhaps salutory to remember how timorous the proposals on tape recording of the Royal Commission on Criminal Procedure now appear – a point that was acknowledged by its chairman when interviewed by the present writer some years ago.[3]

Provided that promises or threats have not been made to suspects off the record and that the interview has not been informally "rehearsed", the tape recording of interviews would appear to benefit all parties: suspects are better protected against oppressive interrogation tactics; police officers are less subject to unfounded allegations of ill-treatment and impropriety; defence and prosecution lawyers are assisted in the preparation of cases, and the courts are in a stronger position to resolve disputes about what actually happened in the interview room. Even if there remain certain problems that need to be tackled, it can now be said with confidence that police interview procedures have been greatly improved with the advent of tape recording.

In the light of these acknowledged benefits, it is surely a sad irony that few of the tapes are being played. The courts almost never listen to them because most cases (if they proceed to court at all) end as guilty pleas, and this means that the way an interview has been conducted is not at issue in the case. Crown Prosecutors concede that they do not bother to play a tape unless the case is to be contested, and, given the pressure of work, see no point in listening to other recordings except in rare circumstances. The author's examination of police records reveals that

---

[1] The debate surrounding the introduction of tape recorders in police stations is discussed at some length in J. Baldwin (1985).
[2] The main problem with the recording of interviews is that its value might be diminished or undermined by off the record exchanges with suspects. For a forceful statement of this view, see M. McConville (1992).
[3] See further J. Baldwin (1986) at pp. 17–18. The Royal Commission on Criminal Procedure (1981), at paras 4.16–4.30, while favourably disposed to the idea of tape recording, recommended that only an officer's oral summary of an interview together with suspects' comments on its accuracy should be recorded.

only a small minority of tapes are ever requested by defence solicitors.[4] Everyone relies instead, in the great majority of instances, on the summary – or "record of interview" – compiled by one of the interviewing police officers. In other words, rather than playing the tapes, the parties are taking on trust what a police officer states in the record of interview.

It is hard to resist the conclusion that some of the main benefits of tape recording interviews with suspects are being frittered away by too heavy a reliance upon the records of interview. It is no exaggeration to say that the success of tape recording procedures as presently operated hinges upon the quality of the summaries. A Home Office Circular in 1988 recognised that the record of taped interview "must always provide an accurate and reliable account of the relevant parts of the interview upon which the Crown Prosecution Service can rely" and stated that:

> The successful introduction of tape recording depends on the provision by the police of an adequate written record of the contents of an interview which is acceptable to the crown prosecutor and the defence – so as to keep to a minimum the need for the tape to be listened to or for a full transcript to be provided.[5]

A Circular issued by the Home Office in 1991 further underlined the importance of the record of interview, identifying its main purpose as being

> to provide a balanced, accurate, and reliable summary of what has been said which contains sufficient information to enable the Crown Prosecutor to decide whether or not a criminal prosecution is appropriate and whether the proposed charges are appropriate.[6]

It is also acknowledged in this Circular that the record of interview will also be used "for the conduct of the case by the prosecution, the defence, and the court where the Record of Taped Interview has been accepted by the defence."[7]

It is, however, well known that the quality of records of interview leaves much to be desired. It is recognised within the police service itself that officers have neither the time nor the aptitude to do the job properly, and few police forces make any claim to do it adequately. The author's

---

[4] Only 69 requests for tapes were made by firms of solicitors out of six hundred cases examined in an earlier study conducted by the author.

[5] Home Office Circular 76/1988, dated August 17 1988, at para. 23.

[6] Home Office Circular 39/1991: Replacement Annex D at para. 2. A later Circular 21/1992 was issued in February 1992 by the Home Office and this contains certain revisions to Annex D. The Circular was issued after the first draft of this report had been completed, although it does not affect in any material way the conclusions that have been drawn.

[7] *ibid*. See also Code of Practice (E) on Tape Recording at para. 5B for a clear statement of the purposes to be fulfilled by the record of interview.

research conducted in the West Midlands in 1989 revealed that a half of the records of interview examined did not provide fair summaries of the interview, and as many as a third contained material that gave a misleading or distorted view of an interview.[8] The main problems uncovered in that research related to the reproduction of meaningless or confusing *verbatim* extracts, the omission of relevant details, inordinate length, and, more generally, a failure to convey adequately the gist of what had been said at an interview.

From conversations with police officers, solicitors and members of the Crown Prosecution Service outside the West Midlands, it seems that things are no better – and may indeed be worse – in other police areas. The preparation of adequate records of interview is now viewed as a national problem, and it seems that the kinds of difficulty identified in 1989 in the West Midlands are being experienced in most other parts of the country as well.

It is not difficult to understand why a high proportion of records of interview fail to meet satisfactory standards. It seems unrealistic to expect that relatively junior police officers (for it is they who conduct the vast majority of interviews with suspects [9]) will have the technical or literary skills needed to master the difficult art of précis. The police service is doing this work simply because no other body is prepared to undertake it, and it is no great surprise to find that it is being done inexpertly and without much enthusiasm. Moreover, there is a natural tendency for police officers to view matters from a prosecution perspective by, for instance, ignoring a suspect's denials or expressions of contrition when constructing the record of interview. The upshot is that the records provide a thoroughly shaky basis for decision making by prosecution and defence lawyers alike. At senior levels of the police service, there is a great deal of anxiety not only about the manpower expended in preparing the summaries but also about the standards that are currently achieved. And much soul-searching is taking place about what might be done to put matters right.

One indication of this concern has been the setting up of various committees to examine the question. A Working Party (consisting of representatives of the Association of Chief Police Officers, the Crown Prosecution Service and the Home Office) recently made a series of recommendations designed to improve the situation, and Home Office Circular 39/1991 was issued as a result. This Circular set out a number of

---

[8] See on this J. Baldwin and J. Bedward (1991).
[9] Almost three quarters of the six hundred interviews examined by the author in his earlier research were conducted by officers of constable rank. In very few cases indeed did an inspector (or more senior officer) interview a suspect: see J. Baldwin (1992).

practical steps designed to simplify the compilation of records of interview. It requires – as does Code of Practice (E) on Tape Recording – *verbatim* reproduction in all cases of questions and answers which contain admissions (whether full, partial or equivocal), and it divides cases into two categories, "complex" and "straightforward." It is stated in the Circular that most cases will fall into the latter category, and, for such cases, a record of interview of not much more than a single page is thought adequate.

The relevance of this dichotomy into complex and straightforward cases is that it is anticipated that for the latter it will be usually appropriate for the record to be written largely in the third person, provided that any admissions and the questions leading up to them are recorded *verbatim*. For complex cases, on the other hand, all the salient points must be recorded *verbatim*, including the suspect's attitude to the offence, possible defences, bail or alternative pleas or charges, though mitigating factors may be summarised in the third person.[10] Consideration will be given later in this report to the extent to which the advice set out in Circular 39/1991 will assist those who prepare records of interview.

The purpose of the present study was to determine whether the difficulties that police forces throughout the country are currently experiencing in compiling accurate and balanced records of interview are remediable. It was not a study of a representative group of forces or of the problems that they currently face; rather it was an attempt to examine the degree of success achieved by the forces which have made the greatest efforts to overcome the difficulties. It was proposed from the outset that four police forces should be studied and that fifty tapes and the corresponding records of interview be examined from each force. Soundings were taken within both the Home Office and the police service to identify those forces which had adopted the most promising approaches in preparing records of interview with a view to including them in the study.

The first point to note here is that, although one hears about the imagination and effort that are being devoted to solving the problems of summarising tape recorded interviews and about the experiments that are taking place to that end, these experiments prove curiously elusive when one sets about locating them. The truth is that little innovation and experimentation are taking place, and most of the forces that were nominated as worth including in this study proved upon examination to be ones in which no special efforts were in fact being made.

---

[10] These points are set out in paragraphs 7–9 of the Circular.

The pilot schemes run by two forces – Northamptonshire and Hampshire – are, however, well known exceptions, and both forces willingly agreed to participate in this study. In Corby in Northamptonshire, a system has been in operation since 1991 in which civilians are used as summarisers and, in Bitterne in Hampshire, civilians have been employed for over three years to type the passages from interviews that police officers have earlier identified (by reference to the tape counter) together with any third person narrative that the officer has added. Both forces have reported substantial savings in the time officers spend on the preparation of summaries as a direct consequence of adopting these methods. An attempt will be made in this report to assess the more important consideration: how good are the records of interview that they produce?

Deciding upon the two other forces to include in the study proved much more difficult, and, after extensive formal and informal consultation, Kingston in the Metropolitan Police District and Leicestershire were selected. The former was nominated by the M.P.D. itself as the division in London which was most likely, because of its traditions and approach, to be capable of producing good quality summaries, and the latter was suggested by the Home Office because the Force was recognised, in the words of a Home Office official, for its "emphasis upon training and its general forward-looking approach." Both forces were willing to participate in the study, and great efforts were made in all four to collect together the samples of tapes and records of interview and to make them available at short notice to the author.[11]

The examination of records of interview

The purpose of the study was to determine whether those police forces which had made the greatest efforts in overcoming the difficulties in preparing records of interview had achieved that objective. The study was in that sense deliberately geared to producing the best possible results.

---

[11] The author is indebted to Mr Mark Thomas of the Administrative Support Unit at Bitterne Police Station; Chief Superintendent Parry and Chief Inspector Vines of the Northamptonshire Police; Superintendent Harris of the Metropolitan Police, and Detective Chief Superintendent Carr of the Leicestershire Police for their efficiency and care in providing samples of tapes and records of interview. All records of interview used in this study related to interviews conducted between July 1990 and December 1991 The selection of cases for inclusion in the samples was determined by the forces concerned on the understanding that they provided a good cross-section of cases. Given the pressures of time, there was no alternative to relying upon the forces providing adequate and representative samples. It might be assumed that, insofar as any of the samples were subject to bias, the distortions would operate so as to show the records of interview in an unduly favourable light.

Given the bleakness of the general landscape, each of the forces included in the study seemed on the surface to offer at least some hope that the difficulties might be surmountable and that they might indicate the appropriate direction in which other forces struggling with the same problem might move.

The procedures adopted in the study were in essence simple. The author played each tape made available by the four forces and formed an assessment of whether the record of interview provided a balanced and accurate summary of the salient points that had emerged in the interview. This inevitably required a subjective judgment insofar as a decision had to be made about whether what had been said in an interview was sufficiently important to be included in the summary, but it was in practice relatively easy to decide on the key points in the great majority of cases. And, since the concern was not over minor omissions or inaccuracies but more fundamental deficiencies, it is doubtful that other people making the assessments would have reached very different conclusions.[12] It was a question of asking whether the document provided a fair summary of an interview which could safely be relied upon by both prosecution and defence as the Home Office Circular requires. In this report, many examples of the deficiencies in the summaries are cited in some detail so that readers can form their own view of the validity of the assessments made by the author.

Table 1: Assessment of the quality of records of interview as fair and balanced summaries of the interviews conducted

	Hants	Kingston	Northants	Leics	Total	%
A reasonable outline of salient points	1	21	21	21	64	32.0
A reasonable outline but much too long	13	5	10	7	35	17.5
Too much relevant detail omitted	17	11	16	14	58	29.0
Misleading, distorted or of poor quality	19	13	3	8	43	21.5
	50	50	50	50	200	100.0

[12] In the author's earlier study in the West Midlands, he and a colleague made the assessments of summaries independently of each other. The two sets of assessments tallied closely in the great majority of cases: see J. Baldwin and J. Bedward (1991). Because of constraints of time in the present study, the view was taken that it would not be practicable to use two assessors.

The results of this exercise reveal that even in the areas in which the greatest efforts have been made, a satisfactory standard is being achieved in only a minority of cases. This is a disappointing conclusion and an attempt will be made later in this report to indicate what is going wrong. The figures presented in the table above give some idea of the main problems that have been experienced.

Table 1 shows that less than a third of all the records of interview examined could be said to provide accurate and succinct summaries of interviews, a figure that is somewhat depressed by the poor showing in Hampshire. A half of the records of interview were deemed unsatisfactory or likely to mislead defence and prosecution lawyers, a proportion that varied from 38 per cent in Northamptonshire to 72 per cent in Hampshire.

Reading the records of interview reveals something of a paradox. While many are lengthy (38 per cent were four or more pages long[13]), some of the longest summaries nevertheless leave out important details relating to the offence itself or the suspect's response to the allegations that are being made. Such omissions may be vital to the defence, and indeed to the prosecution, in making decisions about the way the case should be handled. In this sample, there were many examples of pages of unimportant detail from one part of an interview being faithfully reproduced, while later stages were entirely omitted, almost as if the summariser had run out of steam.

Decisions about what needs to be included in a summary, what needs to be reproduced *verbatim* and what can safely be left out caused the greatest difficulty in all areas. In Bitterne in Hampshire, where the most disappointing results were found, the basic problem was that, while lengthy passages were extracted from many interviews (providing full transcripts of those parts of the interview), reference to other important information that emerged elsewhere in the interview was in most cases entirely omitted. In other words, most records of interview consisted of chunks of an interview written out *verbatim* with little, if any, linking narrative offered by the officer.

In these circumstances, the basic problem relates to the judgment that is being exercised by officers in determining what should be included and what should not, coupled with their general disinclination to provide passages of narrative that might link together those passages that have been transcribed. In no more than fourteen of the fifty records of

---

[13] Comparisons between the forces included in the study are difficult since 64 per cent of the records in Kingston and 38 per cent in Leicestershire were handwritten. All records in the other forces were typed.

interview in Bitterne had police officers included any linking or summarising narrative at all in the summary. The other records consisted exclusively of *verbatim* extracts, apart from an opening sentence, repeated in virtually all Bitterne cases, which glibly reads "The defendant was cautioned and it was established that the defendant was happy to be interviewed in the absence of a solicitor."[14] And even when officers added their own piece of narrative, it exceeded four lines in only three of the fifty cases.

Although this serious flaw was also found in the other areas, it was nevertheless in Hampshire that the problem was particularly acute. It is odd that it should arise so frequently in the Force that has made the greatest effort to overcome it, and it may be helpful to consider examples from Hampshire of the kind of omissions that are seriously affecting the quality of the records of interview.[15]

Case 1 (Hampshire) This is a minor theft case and the summary consists entirely of *verbatim* quotes from the interview chosen idiosyncratically. It is difficult to see why all this material needs to be reproduced. It is a very simple interview and most of the summary relates to the first four minutes. One admission and a very important denial are omitted. No mention is made of the suspect's denial and confusion in the last five minutes. It is a serious distortion of what happened in the interview.

Case 8 (Hampshire) This summary is twelve pages long and relates to the taking of a number of cars. Much of the interview is reproduced *verbatim*. But there is no rhyme or reason to what is included and what is not. It is difficult to make sense of the various offences involved since there is no linking narrative. Whole chunks of the interview are reproduced as transcripts, but the rest is entirely excluded.

Case 9 (Hampshire) This is a very simple case of shoplifting, and it is strange that, in a full record of much of the interview, the crucial detail about whether the suspect intended to return to the shop has been left out. He says in the interview that he thought he had "got away with it" and, since that is omitted from the record of interview, his admission to theft seems equivocal. That statement would be of particular assistance to the prosecution.

Case 11 (Hampshire) It is odd that the suspect's first full admission is omitted as is reference to the scuffle involving the suspect and his friends when arrested. There is also an important point in mitigation about his

---

[14] In only eight of the fifty cases from Bitterne was a lawyer present at the interview.
[15] In these and subsequent extracts from the records of interview, minor details have been altered to ensure anonymity for all parties.

friends trying to persuade him to escape before he gave himself up, and this is again excluded from the summary. The summary also makes no mention of the fact that he had been drinking, that the value of the goods was only £4 and that he volunteers an apology at the end of the interview. Since it is a straightforward shoplifting case, it could hardly be a simpler one to summarise.

Case 20 (Hampshire) The summary, which relates to a case of going equipped for theft, consists of a few carefully selected quotes. But it omits several important details, such as that the suspect is in debt and fearful of being attacked by those to whom he owes money, that other youths were seen armed with various tools and that he denies being with them, and that he denies going equipped to break into cars.

Case 26 (Hampshire) The summary relates to a number of thefts from cars. It covers only the first third of the interview and there is a *verbatim* statement of the suspect's admission in the first part of the interview. However, no reference is made to the discussion initiated by the officer of offences that might be taken into consideration or of the suspect's assertion that he has not been involved in any other offences.

Case 35 (Hampshire) The preparation of seventeen typed pages in a relatively minor theft case seems an incredible waste of effort. Even so, the six minutes of the interview that are omitted are just as relevant as any of the rest – perhaps more so. The exchanges in the final three minutes, when the stolen cheque books are discussed and various denials are made, are omitted. The summary also excludes the discussion of the cannabis found at the suspect's house. This is an odd omission since he admits that it was his. His statement at the end of the interview that it was a "mistake" to buy the car and that it won't happen again is also excluded from the summary.

Case 38 (Hampshire) The thirteen page typed summary includes vastly excessive reproduction of *verbatim* material relating to the suspect's background. The passages that are omitted seem just as important as those included. A crucial passage about whether he threatened his wife with a knife (when other mitigating factors are discussed) is omitted. The final seven minutes of the interview when the knife is discussed further are also excluded from the summary.

The system that has been adopted in Bitterne works unsatisfactorily, then, because too often a crucial step in the procedure is not taken. The police officers who identify the key passages that need to be typed out *verbatim* do not include (as they are instructed to do in the excellent training video produced by the Hampshire Constabulary) summarising narrative of remaining parts of the interview. This means that important parts of an interview which may not need to be reproduced in full, covering perhaps mitigating factors or clarifying the details of an offence, are omitted.

This all-or-nothing approach is not adopted in Northamptonshire, and it is apparent from Table 1 that fewer problems of distortion arose in this Force than in the others included in the study. On balance, Northamptonshire is producing reliable summaries in a higher proportion of cases than in the other areas, yet the success of its approach is reduced by the adoption of a rather curious procedure that was not encountered to anything like the same extent in any of the other forces. This concerns the practice of summarising fully one part of an interview, but covering other important and substantial sections with a reference only to "other matters" being discussed. No details at all are given as to what these matters concern, and it is only by playing the tapes that one can discover how important they are.

In a quarter of the Northamptonshire summaries (compared to only seven per cent of the summaries in the other force areas), it was clear that these "other matters" were very important indeed, and included admissions or denials to other offences, clarification of the particular offence under discussion and suspects' responses to other evidence linking them to the offence. It is worthwhile considering a few typical examples of this phenomenon:

Case 3 (Northamptonshire) The record of interview is of a high standard, with fairly long, but sensibly chosen, *verbatim* quotes. However, there are twelve minutes of the interview, referred to only as "other matters were discussed", in which a number of other offences involving the same complainant are dealt with. Other salient details, including what happened to the property stolen in the burglary, are also omitted.

Case 25 (Northamptonshire) There is a good account of the first five minutes of the interview. The following thirteen minutes are covered by the reference "other matters were discussed", and this means that details of the extensive damage caused to the car, whether the suspect had taken other cars or stolen from cars or committed other offences, are not included in the summary. Just because he denies involvement in other offences does not mean that details of this discussion are not relevant or should not be included in the summary.

Case 30 (Northamptonshire) The final 33 minutes of a 45 minute interview are covered by the single sentence "He was then spoken to regarding other matters." In these 33 minutes, a number of important matters are discussed, including the fact that the suspect was hiding when officers called to his house, other offences he may have committed, the drugs that were found at his house (which he admits possessing) and other evidence that links him to the present offence of stealing a car.

Case 50 (Northamptonshire) Several chunks of the interview are covered only by reference to "discussion took place regarding other matters." These discussions concern offences of taking motor cars (the same offence as that under discussion at the interview), and, while the record of interview is too lengthy in other respects, it omits some crucial admissions.

The adoption of the practice of summarising whole parts of an interview merely as "other matters" means that only a portion of many interviews (sometimes a minor one in terms of time) is summarised, and crucial details of the offence at issue are left out of the summary as a result.[16]

In Hampshire and in Northamptonshire, much *verbatim* material is included in most summaries which could easily be presented in third person narrative form or even excluded altogether. The tendency to err on the side of including too much *verbatim* material rather than too little occurs presumably because it is the typist's and not the officers' time that is wasted. This suggests that insufficient care is being taken in discriminating between parts of an interview that need to be included *verbatim* and other parts that can be summarised or omitted. Much more parsimonious use could without loss be made of *verbatim* materials in all force areas, and this applies particularly in Hampshire and Northamptonshire.

It must also be borne in mind that not all interviews present equal difficulty to summarisers. Long unfocused discussions present more severe problems than do short and simple interviews. It is worth noting in passing that police interviewing is in only a small proportion of cases a protracted affair. At the stations included in this study, 85 per cent of

---

[16] The Northamptonshire Police informed the author that the "tape summarising methodology is based upon advice and training by the Crown Prosecution Service" and that the practice of referring to "other matters" in the records of interview is "reflective of their advice and is acceptable to them." Such advice would seem, however, to be out of line with the 1991 Home Office Circular, a point that is strongly reinforced in Home Office Circular 22/1992. Paragraph 4 of the latter sets out in some detail the requirements relating to offences taken into consideration. Although it is accepted in the Circular that it would be "impracticable" to record *verbatim* all admissions to offences to be taken into consideration, the point is made clearly that:

"The CPS nevertheless need a very clear idea of the offences likely to be taken into consideration, partly to enable them to judge whether the most appropriate offence or offences have been chosen for prosecution and partly to help them to prepare the prosecution case in the knowledge of all relevant circumstances."

interviews took less than half an hour, and a quarter less than ten minutes. They were not, then, the sort of interviews that should have presented inordinate difficulties to summarisers.

The following table shows that summarisers performed significantly better in preparing adequate records of interview where interviews were less than ten minutes long and that the difficulties mounted more or less in direct proportion to the length of the interview. This meant that as many as sixty per cent of all interviews which lasted over twenty minutes were poorly summarised – a proportion that rises to eighty per cent if unduly lengthy summaries are included. Although some of the proportions in the following table are distorted because of the small numbers in some of the categories, there is nonetheless a statistically significant trend for shorter interviews to be better summarised than longer.[17]

Table 2: The relation between the adequacy of the records of interview and the length of the interview

% of records presenting a reasonable outline of salient points

	Hants	Kingston	Northants	Leics	Total
10 minutes or less	9.1	58.8	91.7	66.7	57.1
11–20 minutes	0.0	28.6	52.9	33.3	28.4
21–30 minutes	0.0	41.7	8.3	31.3	20.4
Over 30 minutes	0.0	–	0.0	46.2	20.0
	2.0	42.0	42.0	42.0	32.0

It is immediately obvious to anyone who examines a pile of records of interview that many are lengthy documents. Yet the Home Office, in paragraph 7 of its Circular 39/1991, states that, since the majority of tape recorded interviews will be straightforward in nature, it is likely that the corresponding records of interview will take no more than one side of a sheet of paper. Few summaries in the forces examined were of the anticipated length. Whether typed or hand-written, only 16 per cent of the records of interview were one page or less, 34 per cent were two pages or less, 36 per cent were over four pages and 6 per cent over ten pages. Many of the records of interview were so long that they were virtual transcripts and could not be regarded as summaries of the interview at all. In each area, there were many examples of what seemed a colossal waste of effort, and many lengthy *verbatim* passages could easily have been excised. It is paradoxical that one of the main arguments put up against tape

---

[17] Table 2 includes only cases classified in Table 1 as "a reasonable outline of salient points" and excludes those summaries which were classified as "much too long". However, the trend in Table 2 remains statistically significant whether or not summaries assessed as adequate but over-long are included.

recording in the early years – that enormous expenditure would be incurred in transcribing tapes for use in court – should now re-surface in this way.[18]

Some of the longest records of interview were found in the simplest and most routine cases, and it was often difficult to see the point of such detail. This tendency was particularly evident with the Bitterne cases, where the method of preparation of the record of interview tends to produce that result. Some officers appeared to find it easier to have almost the whole interview transcribed than to bother to identify relevant passages for subsequent reproduction. There were several examples in Bitterne (and elsewhere) of cautions and discussions with suspects about lawyers being present being reproduced *verbatim* in the record of interview.

Prosecutorial biases

The painstaking and needless transcription of materials is not, however, a serious problem, except for those whose time is wasted. Readers can treat such information in the way that they think appropriate and no one is likely to be misled as a result. It is certainly preferable to have too much information rather than too little. The more important question is whether decisions about the material to be excluded from a summary are being made fairly or in ways that favour one side or the other. If, as has already been seen, a half of all summaries cannot be regarded as fair and balanced accounts of what took place in the interview, one must ask whether any biases favour the defence or the prosecution. Are the records of interview, in short, prepared in such a way that they are in effect prosecution summaries?

This is a tricky question to answer since a judgment needs to be made as to the likely consequences of selectivity on the part of the summariser. This said, it is obvious from examining this sample of records of interview that, where biases are present in a summary, they are much more likely to mean that the summary is slanted towards the prosecution than towards the defence. The only exception to this tendency arose in Northamptonshire, where inadequacies in the record of interview seemed to favour the prosecution and defence in roughly equal numbers. In the other three forces, where biases were present in a summary, it was about three times more likely that they would favour the prosecution rather than the defence. Many police officers experience, as one Chief Crown Prosecutor put it to the author, "a mental block when it comes to putting down anything that is favourable to the defendant." The following

---

[18] See further on this point J. Baldwin and J. Bedward (1991) at p. 675.

examples of what is omitted from the summaries indicate that, more often than not, such omissions serve to strengthen the prosecution's case. They also illustrate the dangers for defence lawyers who take such records on trust:

Case 3 (Hampshire) The first half of the interview, which is concerned with an allegation of assault, is intelligently transcribed with relevant questions and answers included. The second half of the interview is, however, omitted from the record. This part deals with some important matters, such as why the suspect failed to cooperate with the police when first arrested, his allegations against the arresting officer, the details of the assault by the arresting officers that he is alleging and the amount he had drunk at the time. The record of interview seems to have been compiled to present the prosecution case only. Most of the suspect's version is omitted.

Case 41 (Hampshire) The summary omits to mention that the suspect has paid for part of the damage he caused and has taken steps to pay for the remainder. These would be very useful points in mitigation.

Case 15 (Kingston) In a twelve page summary containing many irrelevancies, it is striking that it ends abruptly and does not make clear that the suspect wants to pay back the money to the man from whom the property was stolen. This is a serious omission, whether her claim is true or not. The crucial last minutes of the interview, in which the emphatic denials are made, are also excluded.

Case 16 (Kingston) The suspect's response to the allegation is omitted in a very short summary. It also fails to include several crucial parts of the interview, relating to his state of drunkenness, the extent of the damage and the fact that he is "pretty sure" that he didn't commit the offence. It is a misleading summary.

Case 21 (Kingston) This is a sloppy summary, almost as if the officer has prepared it without bothering to re-play the tape. The complexities of the suspect's admissions (he admits stealing some items of property but not others) are not conveyed in the summary. A number of separate burglaries are discussed but the details are not given.

Case 31 (Kingston) Several of the suspect's emphatic denials to allegations of indecent assault are omitted and no flavour of his indignation is conveyed. The summary gives a misleading impression of the suspect's position and attitude, and there seem several subtle omissions as if an attempt is being made to show him in a poorer light than is warranted by the interview.

Case 50 (Kingston) The summary gives details only of the suspect's admissions to possessing cannabis and does not mention the extent to which he assisted the police officers or his final apology.

Case 41 (Northamptonshire) The summary does not convey the suspect's emphatic denials, particularly the fact that he did not run away from the scene as did the other boys – a point that the police officer concedes in the interview. Lengthy passages of the interview are reproduced *verbatim*, yet his indignant denials to the allegations of handling are not adequately reproduced. Given the length of the summary, more information about his attitude should have been provided and more weight given to his denials.

Case 19 (Leicestershire) The record of interview covers only the first seven minutes of an interview that lasts over half an hour, and this means that several important matters are left out. These include discussion of the planning of the burglary, the suspect's strenuous denials that he has committed other burglaries, the fact that his house has been searched and no property recovered from it, and his denial to allegations of drug taking at his house.

Case 37 (Leicestershire) The summary omits to mention the claim by the suspect that it is her current domestic difficulties that led to the burglary offence and that she has been involved in no other offences. She is adamant on this latter point.

Case 48 (Leicestershire) There is much needless reproduction of *verbatim* material in a nine page summary concerned with a serious assault. Considerably more is reproduced of what the officers say than the suspect. The summary omits his expression of remorse, even though the interviewer invites him to express it at the end of the interview because, he says, the tape will be transcribed.

As these comments suggest, there are fundamental biases and omissions in many records of interview, and it would certainly be hazardous for anyone, particularly a defence solicitor, to put much reliance upon them. Despite the great efforts made in each of these forces, the information presented in a half of all the summaries examined cannot be considered a fair reflection of what the suspect said in the interview room. This is too high a proportion to be acceptable, and it indicates that it may not be nearly as easy to remedy the deficiencies in the records of interview as has been assumed in official circles. One can speculate about whether the content of records of interview is deliberately distorted or merely reflects a lack of training and aptitude amongst police officers for preparing a précis of difficult and complex materials. After having discussed the issue with many police officers and lawyers and having examined hundreds of tapes and summaries in this and in an earlier study, the author is extremely doubtful about how far the unfortunate situation that has been described in this report might be retrieved.

Home Office Circular 39/1991

It has already been noted that a Home Office Circular, dealing with the compilation of records of interview, was issued in mid-1991, and it is pertinent to ponder upon whether matters are likely to improve if the advice offered in that document were taken to heart. In the light of the observations made earlier in this report, there can be no real optimism about this, and in the present writer's view the prescription set out in Circular 39/1991 may well serve only to exacerbate the difficulties. It has been a recurrent complaint amongst senior police officers that there has been a lack of clarity in the past in the guidance offered to police forces about how records should be compiled. As one Assistant Chief Constable put it to the author:

> "Some of the responsibility for the confusion in the minds of many police officers about what is, or is not, required to be included in the record of interview is down to those involved in drafting the original Codes of Practice and Home Office Circular and the preparation of the training video."[19]

There are a number of reasons for anticipating that the latest Circular will merely add to this confusion.

These reasons relate to a number of false assumptions and unrealistic expectations upon which the Circular appears to have been based.[20] First, the distinction drawn between "straightforward" and "complex" cases is likely to create serious problems. Even in cases categorised as "straightforward" (for which a one page summary is considered likely to be adequate), the Circular states that, while it will usually be appropriate for the summary to be written largely in the third person, it nevertheless requires that "*any admissions and the questions leading up to them are recorded verbatim*" (para 7 – emphasis in the Circular). In a high proportion of the cases examined in this study,

---

[19] This is a reference to the video, "Getting the Record Straight", which was prepared in 1988 by the Home Office in conjunction with the Association of Chief Police Officers and the Crown Prosecution Service. (For some criticisms of this video, see J. Baldwin and J. Bedward, 1991, at p. 672). A new video was subsequently prepared by the Home Office and this was distributed to all forces in the spring of 1992, together with a new training package.

[20] Most of the records of interview examined in this study pre-date the Circular, but it was possible to identify a number of likely pitfalls even before it took effect in forces throughout the country.

admissions (and accompanying questions) formed a central and lengthy part of interviews and could not possibly be covered on a single sheet of paper if the summariser were to do full justice to them.

Secondly, Circular 39/1991 requires in the writer's view far too much material to be reproduced *verbatim* – admissions in straightforward cases, the main salient points (together with any admissions) in complex cases. Police interviews are often rambling and unstructured encounters and the participants do not invariably speak in clear well-constructed sentences. In some summaries, the relevant passages are transcribed with such fidelity as to make understanding well nigh impossible. Admissions which may be reasonably comprehensible on tape can be very confusing to a reader, even to the point of being turned into near gibberish, when transposed to the written page. The following examples give some impression of the confusion that can be generated:

Case 48 (Hampshire) "Well basically it's a case of criminal damage. Somebody interfered with a friend of mine, and the child's broke into his house, basically three of them with knives and weapons, so I got a bit annoyed and I sort of, well, I damaged somebody's car involved in the incident."

Case 27 (Northamptonshire) "Next minute he came over, he came over and turned round, I turned round and went all right and he went like that, who are you looking at, and that's when he whacked me. He started a big fight in there and next minute I knew all the people in there are all around me."

Case 43 (Leicestershire) "You know where the school is, you know as you go down the hill you've got like traffic lights haven't you, not the one, like they've got two aint they, they've got one up near the avenue then you've got one up the road a bit well it was up there it was parked on the side I got one from there last time."

By requiring the transcription of so much *verbatim* material, the Circular will encourage the production of long, repetitive and potentially confusing documents. This point applies with equal force to "straightforward" and "complex" cases.

Thirdly, it is not true to assert, as the Circular does, that "the majority of tape recorded interviews will fall into the straightforward category" (para 7). The exclusion from this category of all cases likely to be heard in the Crown Court, all allegations of assault and cases in which no admissions are forthcoming means that only a minority are left. In the present samples, no more than forty per cent of cases would have been classified as straightforward – a proportion that is fairly consistent in each of the four forces.[21] This means that, in sixty per cent of cases in these samples, full records of interview would need to be prepared, giving *verbatim* details of "the suspect's attitude to the offence, any questioning of or statements by the suspect concerning intent, dishonesty, possible defences, the granting of bail or discussions concerning alternative pleas or charges" (para 8). There is no necessary relationship between the seriousness of offences and their complexity as defined in the Circular, and many of the cases in the present sample that would have been classified as "complex" were relatively trivial in nature. In such cases, it is difficult to understand why so much detail needs to be included, and it seems inevitable that a great deal of police time will be wasted – more than at present in the author's judgment – to enable "the Crown Prosecutor to make an independent decision as to whether prosecution is justified" (para 9). Much of this time could be saved if Crown Prosecutors could be persuaded to play the original tapes more frequently, and, since the records of interview are so often unreliable, there would be other substantial gains to be derived by their doing so. [22]

Finally, the advice given in paragraph 4 of the Circular that officers "should note during the interview the counter times at which anything was said which might later need to be retrieved for verbatim recording or in order to check the accuracy of third person reporting" will surely be unworkable. Counter times will need to be noted for "any admissions, all salient points, aggravating factors and any matters that tell in favour of the accused." This is a demanding, perhaps an impossible, task, even for an officer who is not directly questioning a suspect. It not only requires a judgment to be made on the spot about what falls into these categories, but it also means that this judgment has to be exercised while the officer is making important assessments and decisions in what is often a very tense situation. The additional task of simultaneously noting counter times is likely only to produce a deterioration in interviewing standards. It is simply impractical to expect interviewers (or even passive colleagues) to do this, and it will further encourage the practice of citing passages out of context. If an accurate record of interview is to be produced, then there is surely no alternative to the officer re-playing the whole tape. This is

---

[21] It is mainly because a substantial proportion of suspects deny involvement in an offence which has not been witnessed by a police officer that a majority of cases have to be classified as "complex."

[22] It is certainly unsatisfactory to argue that the Crown Prosecution Service is able to provide a check on standards by returning inadequate records of interview to the police officer and ask that the exercise be repeated. Without playing the tape, Crown Prosecutors cannot know whether a record of interview is adequate or not, and at present it seems that they rarely request that summaries be rewritten. One Crown Prosecutor told the author that this would only be done where a summary was "glaringly dreadful."

particularly important when, as often happens, a significant amount of time has elapsed before the record is prepared.

It is for these reasons that one greeted with some scepticism the publication in February 1992 of a fresh set of guidelines from the Home Office. The new Circular 21/1992 revises and refines the guidance that was offered in earlier Circulars, providing further advice on such matters as when *verbatim* material is necessary and how offences to be taken into consideration should be dealt with. Although the new Circular contains some useful advice to summarisers, it is unlikely that the mere provision of further guidance will produce any improvement in the grim situation described in this report. On the contrary, it seems predictable that the new set of guidelines will result in even greater confusion, unduly protracted records and a massive increase in police time expended on the task.

Conclusion

The picture that has emerged from this study is bleak. Even the most progressive forces in the country are failing to produce good quality records of interview in a sufficiently high proportion of cases. Furthermore, the guidance from the Home Office on the subject appears to be unpromising. In tackling the difficulties of compiling balanced records of interview, there is no easy solution and, after years of endeavour, one must surely now be pessimistic about the ability of the police service consistently to prepare records of interview up to the standard required.

The results of this study, which closely parallel those of the author's earlier study in the West Midlands, indicate that there is about a fifty per cent chance that any record of interview will be faulty or misleading – a proportion that increases with the length of interviews. In this study, assessments of the quality of records of interview have been made with a certain charity, and this means that, if anything, it presents the summaries in an unduly favourable light. Yet even when imaginative approaches are examined, records of interview remain dangerously flawed in a high percentage of all cases. There seem to be fundamental and inherent difficulties that undermine the usefulness of the records of interview prepared by police officers.

There are, however, some crumbs of comfort. If police officers are to continue to be required to produce the records of interview, then one might derive some consolation from the fact that the approaches adopted both in Bitterne and in Northamptonshire probably indicate the best ways of going about it. If the deficiencies noted in this report that arose in these areas were remedied, then standards could be significantly raised. It is easy to see how improvements could be made if greater care were taken in identifying relevant passages for transcription and if the records of interview did not focus on narrowly defined parts of an interview. Even so, it must be recognised that the main attractions of both approaches – that they will produce savings in police manpower – tend to encourage this kind of corner cutting.

There is unlikely to be any final solution to the problems that have been identified in compiling balanced and fair records of interview. Police officers' summaries are for a variety of reasons almost inevitably flawed in a substantial proportion of cases. It seems unrealistic to expect that police officers, who possess a wide range of literary abilities, will be able to produce the type of balanced and succinct summary that is needed. It is too tall an order for any group, and it is clear that police officers are not well suited to it. It became increasingly evident in carrying out the present study that police officers, because of their temperament, aptitude, educational background, tradition and training, are unlikely to be predisposed to summarise complex materials in a way that can safely be relied upon by other parties. The solution seems not to lie in more police training, and it is unlikely that Circulars from the Home Office, however carefully drafted, can do much to improve matters.

The inherent difficulties of preparing an accurate précis are compounded by the need to exercise sound judgment about what can be left out without distortion, and, the more summaries that one examines, the more convinced one becomes that police officers suffer from an understandable, and probably ineradicable, tendency to view matters through a prosecution prism. The compilation of summaries is not a neutral fact-gathering exercise but one that depends on intuitive judgment. In consequence the scope for conscious and unconscious bias (not to mention more subtle attempts at distortion) is infinite.

While the task remains the responsibility of the police service, it seems inevitable that such problems will arise. Where the interview forms an important part of the prosecution case – and in many cases it is the crux – it is surely unprofessional for lawyers (particularly defence lawyers) to take police officers' summaries on trust. It is not simply that officers may not have the aptitude or the ability to prepare such documents adequately or that they may seek to slant them in favour of the prosecution: it is rather a matter of lawyers in an adversarial system performing their own roles professionally. It is surely incumbent upon defence lawyers, particularly where they have not themselves been in attendance at the police station, to play the tape.[23]

---

[23] The argument sometimes advanced that defence solicitors, who have not attended an interview, can check the accuracy of the summary with their clients is not satisfactory. It is unrealistic to expect a suspect, perhaps weeks after the event, to be able to confirm that the summary is accurate, still less to be able to identify any omissions or to appreciate the legal significance of what was said at the time.

There is in the author's view no effective substitute for the lawyers involved in criminal cases taking the time to do this in a much higher proportion of cases than happens at present. As noted earlier in this report, most interviews are relatively short, and the tapes provide the best picture available of what has taken place in the interview room. It has to be recognised that such a move would have important resource implications, and it is extremely doubtful whether an overstretched Crown Prosecution Service would be able to cope with the added burden of playing tapes without an increase in manpower. Yet, if Crown Prosecutors are to carry out their most critical function effectively – that of case review in order to decide on the appropriate course of action – then playing the tape must be regarded as a central and unavoidable part of that function.

The compromise of involving civilians in the process, as happens in Bitterne and Northamptonshire, indicates a possible direction for progress, although this solution is unlikely to be one that appeals to all police forces. Even when adopted, more determined efforts will need to be made in the future to ensure that the civilians concerned are themselves adequately trained, and, no less important, that they have fully absorbed the legal significance of what is required in these documents. An ability in the art of précis is a necessary, but not a sufficient, qualification for this work. And it is important to remember that, whether civilians or police officers carry out the work, active supervision and monitoring need to be provided within the police service. Senior officers at the stations included in this study could have spotted any of the deficiencies in records of interview noted by the present writer. Such supervision would appear to be a rarity in the police service at present, yet, without it, it is extremely doubtful that much progress will be made in improving overall standards.[24] But these solutions are unlikely to prove more than palliatives. It is simply unrealistic to expect police officers, of whatever rank, to collect and prepare evidence in an adversarial fashion and then present neutral summaries of the taped interview in ways that will be helpful to both prosecution and defence.

The message of this report is clear: there is no satisfactory alternative to lawyers using the record of interview only after having played the tape itself. This should not be looked on as a purist's solution or as impractical and prohibitively expensive: it is rather the only sure way of avoiding the high risk strategy of taking the records of interview on trust – and the odds at present are greatly inferior to those that apply in Russian roulette. If this conclusion is justified in the four police forces

---

[24] The Home Office Circular 21/1992 places great emphasis upon senior officers monitoring the quality of records of interview. It recommends that supervisors be encouraged to listen to a selection of tapes and compare their contents with the relevant records (para. 7).

which have made the greatest efforts to overcome the problems, then it surely applies even more strongly elsewhere. The expenditure of lawyers' time will mean that records of interview can return to being genuine summaries rather than transcripts, and there will be substantial savings of police officers' time as a result. More important, the lawyers can then be confident – in a way that is certainly not possible at present – that their decision making is soundly based.

THE ROLE OF LEGAL REPRESENTATIVES AT POLICE STATIONS

JOHN BALDWIN

Introduction

The 1984 Police and Criminal Evidence Act provides that suspects in police custody may at any time consult privately with a lawyer, and legal advice is now provided free of charge to suspects regardless of their means.[1] Although fears continue to be expressed that suspects are discouraged from asserting these rights and criticisms made that too many solicitors are reluctant to turn up at police stations,[2] there is nevertheless a good deal of research evidence which shows that much higher proportions of police interviews are now conducted in the presence of a lawyer than was the case a decade ago.[3]

Little is known about the role that lawyers actually play in interviews, however, and an opportunity was presented to the present writer to examine this question in some detail in a study which started in 1989 concerned with the video recording of police interviews with criminal suspects.[4] This study covered four hundred video recorded interviews – a hundred drawn from each of four police stations: the Belgrave Road and Wednesfield stations in the West Midlands, Redditch in West Mercia and Edmonton in the Metropolitan Police District. Two hundred audio recordings taken from two stations in Birmingham – Kings Heath and Bournville Lane – were also examined and comparisons drawn with the video recordings. All six hundred interviews were recorded in the period between October 1989 and November 1990. Although it cannot be claimed that these cases represent a scientifically selected sample of interviews,[5] the tapes have nonetheless provided a wealth of information about how interviews with suspects are being conducted and have covered

---

[1] The only exception, albeit an important one, arises where suspects have been detained in connection with a "serious arrestable offence": see Code of Practice for the Detention, Treatment and Questioning of Persons by Police Officers (Code C) at paras 6.1–6.15 and Annex B.

[2] See, for instance, A. Sanders, L. Bridges, A. Mulvaney and G. Crozier (1989); K. Bottomley, C. Coleman, D. Dixon, M. Gill and D. Wall (1990), and D. Wolchover and A. Heaton-Armstrong (1991).

[3] The available research evidence indicates that a legal representative is in attendance in about a third of all interviews. There are, however, wide variations from study to study and from station to station in the proportions noted: see further D. Brown (1989) at pp 19–36.

[4] This study has been funded since 1989 in the West Midlands by the Leverhulme Trust and since 1990 in West Mercia and London by the Home Office. I am indebted to the Royal Commission on Criminal Justice for its subvention which has enabled interviews with legal advisers to be conducted.

[5] If, for example, individual officers chose not to make use of the video equipment, they in effect excluded themselves from the sample.

matters of all grades of seriousness and involved hundreds of different interviewers.

Examining these recordings gives a good idea of the role that is played by legal representatives at these interviews in different parts of the country. The proportion of legal representatives who attended interviews varied widely from station to station. It was as high as fifty per cent at the Belgrave Road station in Birmingham but only 17 per cent in Redditch. Of the six hundred interviews examined, 182 (30.3 per cent) involved legal representatives. This study focuses on the role that was played by legal advisers in the interviews in question.

The role of legal representatives at interviews

The most striking point to emerge from the recordings is the general passivity of legal representatives at the interviews. They may or may not have given the suspect forceful advice before the interview started, but the great majority said little, if anything, in the course of the interview itself. When they did intervene, it was as likely to be to facilitate police questioning as to push their clients' interests. In a few cases, indeed, they virtually played the role of a third interviewer, and one strange benefit of having interviews on video tapes is that it enables one to see whether it is a police officer or a solicitor who is putting questions to a suspect. The following table summarises the role that lawyers were seen to play at interviews at each station included in the study.

Table 1: Role played by legal representatives in interviews

	Bournville	Kings Heath	Belgrave Rd	Wednesfield	Edmonton	Redditch	Total	%
Says nothing in interview	17	19	27	19	29	10	121	66.5
Clarifies minor matters	1	4	6	1	1	2	15	8.2
Clarifies important matters	1	2	1	0	1	2	7	3.8
Pushes suspect's interests	0	0	4	3	4	3	14	7.7
Is obstructive	0	0	2	0	1	0	3	1.7
Plays role of third interviewer	5	3	8	0	0	0	16	8.8
Other type of role	2	0	2	2	0	0	6	3.3
No lawyer present	74	72	50	75	64	83	418	—
	100	100	100	100	100	100	600	100.0

It is evident, then, that few of the legal representatives who were present at these interviews could be described as obstructive or interventionist in the approach that they assumed. Hostility towards the interviewing officers was virtually unknown, and, although there is provision in the Code of Practice for expelling representatives from an interview room if their conduct is such that an interviewer is unable properly to put questions to a suspect,[6] this did not arise in any of the interviews in the samples.

The crucial question is, therefore, whether legal representatives ought to have intervened more often than they did in these interviews. This is obviously a difficult question to answer with any precision, since the appropriate role for a lawyer to play is not clearcut but is left largely to an individual's interpretation and judgment. It is not the purpose in this report to discuss the propriety of police questioning, since it is a vast and complex subject.[7] Suffice it to say that, in the six hundred cases included in this study, there were many in which in the view of the author some intervention on the part of the legal representative was called for. In many instances lawyers sat in silence when the situation seemed to cry out for them to intervene or to raise some objection to the nature of the questioning. The following are a few examples of the sort of cases in which legal representatives might have been expected to intervene.[8]

Case 43 (Bournville Lane) This comes across as an unfair interview in that the police officers appear to assume guilt in what is a complex domestic situation. They do not attempt to get the suspect's side of the story but simply assume that he is in the wrong. At one point they get a significant detail of the evidence wrong, having misunderstood a statement, and decline to apologise to the suspect in the face of his indignant response. On several occasions the officers lose control of the interview, and their basic mistake is to assume a black and white situation when matters are obviously much less clearly defined. They appear not to listen to what the suspect says, and there are several points in the interview when the officers are themselves confused about the details when one might have expected a solicitor to clarify matters.

Case 15 (Kings Heath) The police officers are confused about many technical matters relating to what they call "very deep Road Traffic law", and they are by no means certain that an offence has even been committed. They ask the suspect if he can confirm that he has in fact

---

[6] See paras 6.9–6.11 in Code C on questioning.
[7] Some results of the analysis of police interviewing methods are given in J. Baldwin (1992) at pp. 9–18.
[8] In some of the cases quoted, minor details have been altered to preserve the anonymity of the individuals involved.

committed the offence, but he wisely declines to do so. The representative who is present makes no attempt to clarify matters.

Case 55 (Kings Heath) One of the interviewers adopts a needlessly harrying tone from the outset. He asks rapid-fire questions and hardly pauses to allow the suspect to answer. The officer's voice gradually rises as the youth denies the allegations that are made. At the end of the interview, the officer, clearly disappointed that no confession has been forthcoming, says sarcastically, "What a joke! What a laugh! That's rubbish, isn't it? Absolute rubbish! Absolute rubbish!" The duty solicitor who is present says nothing in the interview even when invited to do so.

Case 12 (Belgrave Road) The interviewers repeatedly tell the suspect that he is lying. It is a tedious interview, going over the same ground time and time again. The officers seem hell-bent on securing an admission and go on and on with the same questions and the same assertions in an interview that lasts over an hour. The questioning is very repetitive, and it is difficult to see why they go to these lengths when the evidence (including strong forensic evidence) is itself compelling. The legal representative says nothing in the interview.

Case 16 (Belgrave Road) The officers clearly do not believe the suspect's explanations and challenge him forcefully throughout. The interview is laboured and tends to go round in circles. The attitude of one of the officers is decidedly unpleasant and he tries repeatedly to catch the suspect out. He has to be corrected by the other officer on one occasion. He has a distasteful tone which is unhelpful and ineffective. The legal representative does not say anything in the interview.

Case 47 (Belgrave Road) This is a poor interview with one of the officers acting aggressively, even to the point of losing his temper with the suspect. There is a disagreeable atmosphere at the interview, with the officers responding in kind to the suspect's unpleasant manner. The solicitor's only intervention is to tell the youth to answer the question rather than nodding his head as the tape cannot pick this up.

Case 54 (Belgrave Road) The tone of the interview changes abruptly as the officer becomes increasingly assertive, repeatedly accusing the suspect of lying, saying that she is behaving in a "despicable" and "terrible" manner. The other officer adopts a more sneering tone, though he too is aggressive towards the woman. Both officers refer to her within the space of a few minutes as "an out-and-out liar." When this approach fails to produce an admission, the suspect is told that she may need "help" and the tone of the interview is shrill and harrying, almost gratuitously offensive. The legal representative says almost nothing in a series of interviews that last almost two hours.

Case 66 (Belgrave Road) The interview becomes increasingly aggressive as the officers tell the suspect that he is continually telling lies. One officer raises his voice, almost shouting at the suspect. It becomes more like an argument than an interview as the suspect himself gets angry. The officers seem intent on "needling" the suspect and are supercilious in the approach they adopt. The legal adviser says nothing whatever in the interview.

Case 12 (Wednesfield) The interviewer is at times needlessly confrontational, and the approach seems to be aimed at wearing down the suspect to prompt a confession. The interview is very repetitive and lasts for over three hours, yet the legal representative says nothing in the course of it.

Case 48 (Wednesfield) One of the officers is much more vigorous and forceful than the other, raising his voice at times, apparently impatient with the youth's answers. He even interrupts the other officer as she is asking a question and they seem to be operating at cross-purposes on several occasions – quite a serious problem in the interview. There are many attempts to catch the suspect out, and it comes close to the officer putting words into the suspect's mouth. In two interviews that last almost eighty minutes, the lawyer says nothing at all.

Case 59 (Wednesfield) The suspect is offered thoroughly misleading information in relation to offences that might be "taken into consideration" in an attempt to induce him to admit to other offences. The officers repeatedly stress that he "won't be punished" for offences taken into consideration, and they fail to stress that he should not admit offences for which he is not responsible. The representative says nothing while this discussion is taking place.

Case 9 (Redditch) The suspect is given an opportunity to put his version of events and he offers a detailed account of what took place. The officers challenge this version with reference to statements that have been made, and the challenge becomes quite stern and tough. They disbelieve his claim that he cannot remember crucial parts of the altercation. One officer raises his voice when the suspect corrects him on whether he slapped or punched the other youth. The following brief exchange then takes place:
Interviewer: "Don't try and be smart."
Suspect: "I'm not trying to be smart, sir."
Interviewer: "Don't try and suggest that I'm getting myself confused."
The interview gets unduly heated, and, having tested the suspect's version repeatedly, it is difficult to see why this tone needs to be adopted with a youth who calls the officer "Sir", has no previous convictions and is cooperative. The officer seems to accept the complainant's version and to

be unwilling to listen to what the suspect says. There is an assumption of guilt and the interview is very repetitive. Compared to the suspect, the officers seem ill-mannered. The legal representative who is present contributes almost nothing to a long interview.

Case 59 (Redditch) The officers struggle to get some information out of a difficult suspect. However, their manner is sarcastic and one officer allows himself to become exasperated by an awkward subject. He seems intent on provoking the suspect and putting him down (e.g. by constant references to him as "mate"). A duty solicitor who is present says nothing, despite one attempt by the suspect to get him to support his position.

Case 96 (Redditch) Both officers are particularly assertive, pointing with their fingers at the suspect, and their manner borders at times on the aggressive. One officer calls the suspect, "a bare-faced liar . . . talking crap, utter rubbish, complete and utter fabrication." Although the suspect is an elderly man, the young detective continually uses his christian name and on several occasions even calls him "son." It is only at the end of two lengthy interviews that the legal representative interrupts to complain about the repetitive nature of the questioning and the pressure that is being put on his client.

Case 80 (Edmonton) The officers are robust in their approach in interviewing a sixteen year old youth about a robbery that has taken place. One officer says that he has committed "a cowardly, filthy, disgusting kind of offence." The legal representative is silent throughout the interview, although the boy's mother is quite forceful and puts up a spirited challenge to the way that the officers are conducting the interview.

The intention in listing these cases is not to indicate that most questioning in police interview rooms is aggressive or tough – which it is not[9] – or to suggest that legal representatives should be intervening at every turn. It is rather to demonstrate that there are many instances (and the above examples could be multiplied) in which representatives might have been expected to have involved themselves in what was taking place. It seemed to the present writer that in many instances more was required of them than mere passive attendance if their clients' interests were to be adequately protected in the police station.

The few instances in which legal representatives played an active part stood out in stark contrast to the rest, and it might be helpful to consider examples of the circumstances in which representatives chose to intervene in interviews:

---

[9] The present writer has been struck more often by the ineptitude of police questioning than by its hostility: see J. Baldwin (1992) at pp. 15–16.

Case 74 (Bournville Lane) The suspect gets very angry and indignant at the questions that the interviewers put to him, but the legal adviser says nothing until the end of the interview when he asks a point in clarification. It is more in the nature of a point assisting the police line of questioning than an attempt to assist his client. It is almost as if the adviser is trying to catch the suspect out. Indeed, one of the police officers thanks him for asking the question.

Case 5 (Belgrave Road) The representative is quite prominent in the interview both facilitating the officers' questioning and offering sound advice to his client. He seems sensible and pragmatic in his approach, helping to make sense of a difficult and complex situation. In one of his client's many extraordinary outbursts, he sternly warns him that he will leave the room "because I can't carry on an interview like this." At the end of the interview, when one of the police officers is struggling unsuccessfully to calm him, the solicitor shouts at his client:

> "Be quiet or else I shall go! Do you want me to help you? I shall walk out if you don't stop this nonsense."

He makes as if to leave, and, when his client begs him to stay, he warns, "Look then, be quiet!" He is much tougher with his client than are the officers, and they are clearly grateful to the solicitor for his efforts.

Case 21 (Belgrave Road) The representative says nothing for over forty minutes of the interview, and then at the end intervenes to say:

> "I think we're going to reach the stage where either you put different questions or I think we're going to have to finish the interview. You've had a fair crack of the whip. I think you're going to have to move on or finish."

The officers immediately terminate the interview.

Case 36 (Belgrave Road) The legal adviser intervenes at times to safeguard his client's interests but at other times he is like a third interviewer. He certainly does a lot in the interview to facilitate the officers' task. There are conspiratorial nods between the lawyer and one of the interviewers (particularly at the end of the interview), and the impression given is of partnership rather than adversariness.

Case 67 (Redditch) The solicitor is very much involved in this interview and contributes constructively throughout. He repeatedly tells the suspect to calm down when he gets angry or is offensive to the interviewers. He offers the suspect support and advice when he breaks down, and he tells him to concentrate on the questions and not worry at that stage about the gravity of the allegations that have been made. He interrupts later in the interview to complain that the suspect is being repeatedly asked to explain the allegations, and he advises the suspect not to answer the questions. He also asks for clarification of two important points that were covered in the interview. His tone is pleasant throughout.

Case 78 (Redditch) A duty solicitor is present and he draws an important distinction between what was "reasonable force" for the suspect and what was reasonable for the other person involved. The officers accept that the solicitor is right on this point.

Case 62 (Edmonton) The legal adviser intervenes in the interview when the officers are pressing the suspect about the offence at issue. He says that his client has denied the offence three times and that is "fair enough". There is a rather sharp exchange at this stage between the officer and the adviser when the latter reiterates the point. There is then a long embarrassed silence. It is evident that the officers have been thrown off their stride by this (not unreasonable) intervention.

It is clear, notwithstanding the relative passivity of representatives in interviews, that police officers generally do not welcome interventions. The Code of Practice tilts the balance of power in the relationship decidedly in favour of the police officers, not just because they can cause a troublesome lawyer to be expelled from the interview room but more particularly because legal representatives have no power to bring an interview to an end. Even if representatives advise their clients to remain silent, police officers can continue to fire questions at the suspect (providing that their questioning does not amount to "oppression").

Confrontation between police officers and lawyers in the interview room is, however, rare. When it does arise, it can be thoroughly unpleasant as in the following two instances, both of which occurred at the Belgrave Road station:

Case 52 There is an abrupt exchange at one point in the interview when the lawyer says that the officers should not persist with a certain line of questioning. The officer responds:

> "No, we won't [leave it at that], I'm afraid. We're interviewing this man. Right? And we're asking him questions and inviting his replies ... We'll continue asking him questions. You can't answer questions for him. You're here to observe and advise him. But if we want to continue questioning him, we'll continue questioning him, if you don't mind."

The lawyer immediately says: "Well, in that case I advise you not to answer any more questions in regard to that matter." The officer states that he is going to ask more questions and it is up to the suspect whether he wishes to answer them or not. He adds, "I'm not really bothered what your solicitor says to you because I'm asking you the questions, and not him."

The suspect declines to answer the questions and a few minutes later the officer terminates the interview. The officer is clearly disgruntled.

Case 57 There are several *contre-temps* between the solicitor and the police officer in a lengthy series of interviews. On one occasion, when the solicitor disputes the officer's version of what was said the previous day, the officer retorts abruptly, "Please don't interrupt me when I'm speaking, Mr Smith. My interview, please, sir. Don't interrupt." The solicitor splutters with indignation that the officer is trying to mislead the suspect but the officer simply ignores this objection.

Such interventions are very much the exception, and in the routine case the video shows that, if legal representatives are present at an interview, most do little more than write out detailed notes of what is taking place. There is as a rule minimal communication between the legal adviser and the suspect once the interview has commenced. It is as if the lawyer is acting as a neutral observer of the proceedings, and very few indeed could be said to be relentlessly pushing their clients' interests.

As will be seen later, it is also a comparative rarity for lawyers to advise their clients to remain silent. Lawyers simply do not see it as their function to obstruct the course of police questioning. Their role is interpreted in practice as an essentially passive one, and hostile interjections are almost unknown. This silent (one might almost say supine) posture is in stark contrast to what happens in the United States where it would be almost unimaginable that a competent practitioner would allow an interview even to commence, let alone see it as proper to assist police interviewers. Indeed, save in federal cases where special considerations may apply, the interrogation of a legally assisted suspect in the United States is virtually a contradiction in terms.[10]

It is important to note that lawyers in this country are hardly encouraged to be assertive by their governing body. In the guidance that solicitors received from the Law Society at the time this study was conducted, the emphasis was not upon confrontation but upon "mutual

---

[10] As one American law professor expressed it to the author:
"In the United States, defence lawyers learn from their first day in Law School that, as soon as they see their client, they tell them not to answer any questions. It doesn't happen at all under the American system that lawyers would help the police. They may be incompetent, they may be stupid, they may not be of much help, but they never assist the police. Once the lawyers are in the process, there's no more interviewing."
Another legal expert said that for any lawyer even to allow an interrogation to continue would indicate conduct so incompetent as to be "disbarrable."

cooperation" with the police, ensuring fair play and generally doing whatever was required to look after the physical welfare of the suspect.[11]

The stance that the Law Society has taken on this matter in recent years has moved one solicitor to observe that "it would be hard to find a more timid exposition of the role of a solicitor" than the advice offered to them by the Law Society.[12] Any enthusiasm to be assertive in an interview is further dampened by the Code of Practice, and some indication of the generally discouraging tone of the Code is given in the following passage:

> ... a solicitor is not guilty of misconduct if he seeks to challenge an improper question to his client or the manner in which it is put or if he advises his client not to reply to particular questions or if he wishes to give his client further legal advice. It is the duty of a solicitor to look after the interests of his client and to advise him without obstructing the interview.[13]

It is clear, therefore, that lawyers in England are not expected or encouraged to intervene frequently or forcefully at police interviews.

The fact that young inexperienced lawyers tend to be over-represented in criminal practice in England, as elsewhere, further inhibits intervention. Junior personnel are no match for an experienced police interviewer. This imbalance is reinforced where, as happens in a majority of instances at present, articled clerks or other unqualified personnel attend police stations instead of senior officials.[14] With growing dissatisfaction voiced within the legal profession about rates of remuneration under criminal legal aid, it is very likely that this trend will accelerate in the future.

Even so, it is important to remember that most interviewing is done by the junior grades in the police service,[15] and it is clear from talking to police interviewers that they feel a certain apprehension at having a lawyer present. Although such officers are less resistant nowadays to having legal

---

[11] See The Law Society, *Advising a Suspect in the Police Station: Guidelines for Solicitors* (2nd Edition, 1988). A third edition of this booklet was published by the Law Society in 1991. The tone of this is less conciliatory and the emphasis upon "mutual cooperation" has been reduced. Since this booklet was published after the main fieldwork in this study had been concluded, reference is made in this report to the second edition since this was the one available to legal representatives at the time the fieldwork was conducted.

[12] J. Mackenzie (1990); see also D. Wright (1986).

[13] Code of Practice C at para. 6D. On the right to legal advice, see paras 6.1–6.17.

[14] See further A. Sanders *et al* (1989) at pp 92–95.

[15] Almost three quarters of the six hundred interviews included in the author's study involved officers of constable rank.

representatives in interviews than was the case in the past,[16] few of them can be described as genuinely enthusiastic about the prospect. Whether they welcome it or not, however, the presence of legal representatives (albeit passive ones) is becoming an increasingly familiar feature of police interviews.

The right to remain silent

It quickly became apparent from conducting interviews with police officers in the present study that they tended to exaggerate the difficulties that legal representatives posed to them.[17] It was common for them to identify solicitors' advice to clients to say nothing as the most serious difficulty they faced. Of the 51 interviews conducted with officers – all of whom were experienced in using video equipment – no fewer than 27 (53 per cent) complained without prompting about "no comment" interviews in which suspects were said to be aided and abetted by solicitors.

The question whether lawyers encourage their clients not to answer police questions is crucial, and it is important to determine how far the fears and complaints that officers express on this score are borne out by what happens inside the interview room. Before examining this in detail, it is worth noting some of the complexities of the term "silence" within the context of police interviewing.

Suspects are not neatly divided into those who answer questions and those who do not, and there are many suspects who are prepared to answer questions but who decline (refuse is too strong a word) to answer a particular question, often one which has no real bearing upon the interview as a whole. Suspects might be reluctant, for example, to give the name of a girl friend (whom they wish not to be involved) or to describe the involvement of a co-accused. Anxieties about being labelled a "grass" are very real and they are well understood on all sides. Yet even in these cases, the gentlest probing often produced the information desired or else an apologetic recognition by the interviewers that the matter should be dropped. To describe this as the exercise of the right to silence is to exaggerate the importance of what is taking place, and the definition of "silence" needs to be examined within the context of the interview as a whole.

---

[16] On the reluctance of police officers to admit solicitors in the pre-P.A.C.E. period, see M. Zander (1972) and J. Baldwin and M. McConville (1979).
[17] Officers who had carried out at least four interviews in each video tape sample were interviewed in the study. 52 officers fell into this category, at least a dozen of whom were drawn from each of the four stations using video equipment. 51 of them (98 per cent) agreed to be interviewed.

Outright refusals to answer questions (or even certain lines of questioning) were comparatively rare. Table 2 shows that, although many suspects declined to answer certain questions, few exercised this right in more than a technical or nominal way. There were no major exceptions to this general trend at any of the six stations included in this study.

Table 2: The extent to which suspects exercised their right to silence at the police station

	Bourn-ville	Kings Heath	Belgrave Rd	Wednes-field	Edmon-ton	Red-ditch	Total	%
Did not arise in interview	79	88	71	81	78	84	481	80.2
Incidental or nominal exercise of right	11	6	13	7	3	6	46	7.7
Refusal to answer a very few questions though suspect basically cooperative	3	2	7	7	8	3	30	5.0
Refusal to answer a significant number of questions	2	2	4	5	7	2	22	3.6
Refusal to answer questions after part of the interview	4	2	3	0	0	2	11	1.8
Full exercise of right to silence	1	0	2	0	4	3	10	1.7
	100	100	100	100	100	100	600	100.0

The question arises as to the extent to which refusals to cooperate in answering police questions are the result of advice received from legal representatives. Genuinely "no comment" interviews are rare, and Table 3 shows that, although suspects are less likely to answer all of the questions put to them by police interviewers when a legal representative is present,[18] it is nonetheless true that, whether a representative is present or not, the issue of the right to silence simply does not arise in the great majority of interviews.

The results of this study refute the view that is widely held by members of all ranks in the police service that "no comment" interviews

---

[18] The question of cause and effect is relevant here since suspects who intend to remain silent might be more likely to seek legal advice.

are becoming commonplace and that lawyers are mainly responsible for producing them.[19] Few representatives appeared to encourage their clients to exercise the right to silence. Indeed, in viewing the tapes of interview, it was surprising that lawyers were prepared to allow certain lines of questioning to proceed to the extent that they did.

Table 3: The extent to which suspects exercised their right to silence at the police station according to whether or not a legal representative was present

	All stations					
	No lawyer	%	With lawyer	%	Total	%
Did not arise in the interview	361	86.4	120	65.9	481	80.2
Incidental or nominal exercise of right	23	5.5	23	12.6	46	7.7
Refusal to answer a very few questions though suspect basically cooperative	14	3.3	16	8.8	30	5.0
Refusal to answer a significant number of questions	7	1.7	15	8.2	22	3.6
Refusal to answer questions after part of the interview	8	1.9	3	1.7	11	1.8
Full exercise of right to silence	5	1.2	5	2.8	10	1.7
	418	100.0	182	100.0	600	100.0

Advising clients whether or not to answer police questions is a tricky matter for legal representatives. It is important to remember that under English law there is nothing improper about a lawyer advising a client not to answer questions. It may well be sensible advice for a lawyer to recommend silence until the details of the prosecution's case are known.[20] Where it is apparent that the prosecution does not have a *prima*

---

[19] This view was to some extent reinforced by the results of the study conducted by S. Moston, G.M. Stephenson and T.N. Williamson (1990) which suggested that only five per cent of suspects without legal advice asserted their right of silence compared to 33 per cent with a representative. This study was influential in the recommendations relating to the right of silence reached by the Home Office (1989). It is, however, difficult to square these results with those of the present study or those of the large-scale study of the P.A.C.E. provisions conducted by members of the University of Hull: see K. Bottomley, C. Coleman, D. Dixon, M. Gill and D. Wall (1991). Doubts have been cast on the methods adopted in the study undertaken by the University of Kent researchers by D. Dixon (1991) at pp 40-41.

[20] On this point, see M. McConville, A. Sanders and R. Leng (1991) chapter 3.

facie case, for instance, then lawyers would be failing in their duty if they did not warn their clients of the dangers of responding to police questioning.

In many cases, however, it will simply not be in the suspect's own interests to decline to answer questions. The Law Society has itself stressed the "substantial mitigating advantages generally of cooperation with the police",[21] and, since as many as a third of all cases included in the samples used in this study were concluded by the police without referral to the Crown Prosecution Service, there are evidently considerable gains to be derived from being seen to be accommodating at that stage. A large proportion of relatively minor offences (particularly those involving juveniles) are dealt with by means of a police "caution",[22] and since this option is only available if the defendant concerned admits involvement in the offence, there are considerable pressures upon suspects to appear compliant and to confess. The possibility that cases might not be taken further than the police station operates in practice, then, as a powerful inducement to many suspects to cooperate with the police and as a disincentive to them to remain silent.

The law relating to the right of silence acts as a further source of inhibition. The right is in reality not nearly as firmly established in English law as is often assumed. The law is equivocal in the extent to which it allows trial judges to make adverse comments about a suspect's refusal to answer questions at the police station, and evidence of a suspect's silence when first questioned can be admitted in evidence at trial. This means that magistrates and juries may draw their own conclusions from an accused's silence at the police station, even if the law clearly states that guilt must not be inferred from it.[23] The right to silence is in that sense relatively weak in England compared to certain other jurisdictions, and Easton (1991) notes its "lukewarm acceptance" into English law.[24] Many judges have clearly been out of sympathy for some years with suspects who exercise their right to remain silent when questioned by the police (particularly when so-called ambush defences are introduced at trial), and it is now established that judges are entitled to comment upon this fact. In the case of Gilbert,[25] for instance, the Court of Appeal explicitly stated that, while no accused can be compelled to speak before trial,

---

[21] Law Society (1988) at p 33.
[22] The proportion of those processed by the police for indictable criminal offences who are cautioned stands at about a third. This varies greatly between age groups: the vast majority of children and young persons nowadays are cautioned by the police instead of being prosecuted compared to about one in seven of all adult males: see Home Office, *Criminal Statistics: England and Wales 1990* (1992) Cm 1935, Tables 5.2 and 5.3.
[23] Good discussions on this point are to be found in K. Greenawalt (1974); D. Dixon (1991); S.M. Easton (1991), and R. Leng (1992).
[24] *ibid.* at p 2.
[25] R. v. *Gilbert* [1977] 66 Cr. App. R. 237.

it is another thing to say that if he chooses to exercise his right of silence, that must not be the subject of any adverse comment to the accused. A judge is entitled to comment on his failure to give evidence.[26]

It is for reasons of this kind that lawyers tend to fight shy not just of advising clients to remain silent before an interview commences but also of interfering overmuch once it has begun. While it is the author's view that legal advisers could without risk to their clients adopt a more forceful stance in many cases, it is by no means invariably in suspects' interests to have their lawyers relentlessly shielding them from police questioning.

Lawyers' relations with the police

That lawyers set great store by fostering harmonious relations with the police was evident in this study. It emerged not only from observations of the tapes of interviews but was also apparent from talking to the lawyers themselves. The same preoccupation has been noted in earlier research on the subject.[27] In the light of all this evidence, it is very strange that police officers seem stubbornly reluctant to view lawyers other than as hostile elements in an interview. It is worth pausing to consider the views expressed to the author by police officers about having solicitors present at interviews in the police station:

Interview 1 (Belgrave Road) "I find solicitors are a big problem. I believe the outcome of an interview can be hindered by solicitors. People are entitled to obtain advice from a solicitor, but from our point of view when offences have been committed and we are sure the person we've got has committed them, then a solicitor can sometimes get in the way. I don't find any problem with the interview itself, but we find that people upon the advice of a solicitor will clam up, and, under instructions from the solicitor, will say nothing. It's everyone's right but, from our point of view, it makes the job difficult."

Interview 15 (Belgrave Road) "I am generally in favour of having a solicitor present in the interview until they start interfering. In the vast

---

[26] Solicitors were also discouraged from advising clients to remain silent in R. v. *Chandler* [1976] 1 W.L.R. 585. In *Chandler*, the Court of Appeal had said that the principle (enunciated in R. v. *Hall* [1971] 1 W.L.R. 298) that silence in the face of an allegation cannot give rise to an inference that the suspect accepted the truth of the accusation, did not apply where a solicitor was present since the suspect and the police officer were then on equal terms. In the recent case of R v *Welch* (Crim. L.R. 1992 p. 368), the Court of Appeal ruled that, where a suspect answered only certain questions, the whole of the dialogue should be admissible.
[27] See, for instance, A Sanders *et al* (1989); B.L. Irving and I.K. McKenzie (1989); K. Bottomley *et al* (1990; 1991), and D. Dixon (1991).

majority of cases, a solicitor will speak to his clients before and they will work out what they are going to say, etc. But we do get the odd solicitor who likes to stick his nose in, when he is really there just to advise his client and to be there as an observer. But a lot of them do like to take over the interview which I don't like. I tell them to be quiet and I have on one occasion had to eject a solicitor from an interview because he was interfering too much."

Interview 7 (Wednesfield) "Having solicitors present at an interview doesn't cause me any concern at all because at the end of the day I'm asking the questions. Half the time the solicitor is there just as much to help you as he is to help his client. The majority are pro-police but there are certain ones that advise their clients to say nothing at all."

Interview 12 (Wednesfield) "The main problem is solicitors because sometimes it's advantageous for their clients not to answer the questions that are put to them. And, if they say to them, 'Don't answer any questions', then we're put to extra work to try to prove or disprove what they're saying when they could answer the questions and give you the answer straight away."

Interview 7 (Redditch) "Our main problem is the right of silence. If they exercise the right of silence, then the whole purpose of an interview is gone. Generally in this town now solicitors are saying to their clients, 'Don't say a word.' And if people don't speak to you, that's it."

Interview 8 (Redditch) "I think you have to start with the fact that perhaps a person doesn't want to say anything. That's a big problem. If he just says 'no comment', obviously you're a bit stuck. But I wouldn't say that having a solicitor in the interview room is a problem, although I don't like solicitors being there. The suspect is not allowed to turn round to speak to his solicitor and the solicitor isn't allowed to tell him what to say. He's just there to ensure that we conduct the interview properly."

Interview 5 (Edmonton) "The main problem nowadays without a shadow of a doubt is the right to silence. I would say a good 75 to 85 per cent of the people that I interview at this police station give a 'no comment' interview or refuse to answer questions altogether. They just sit there blank-faced, sometimes even to the point where they won't give you their name or address. Once you have a solicitor there, you will invariably get a 'no comment' interview. As soon as someone wants a solicitor, you more or less resign yourself to thinking, 'How else am I going to prove this case?' because you know this bloke is going to come across with a 'no comment' interview. When you deal with cases day after day, then that's the way you look at it."

Interview 6 (Edmonton) "People are very loath to talk to the police. I would think that's the most difficult situation. People come in and say nothing whatsoever. The majority of solicitors come out with the easiest advice which is to say nothing. This gives them a chance to look over all the papers and fight the case on something they can put together at a later occasion. The majority of times the solicitor advises them to say nothing at all and the nature of the interview is completely gone. We all know there is an inalienable right to this silence. It's told to a person on many occasions at a police station. The solicitor seems to reinforce that to such an extent to say it's actually in their interests to say nothing at all. They ruin lots and lots of interviews."

These comments illustrate one feature of police interviewing in England that has continually struck this writer while conducting research on the subject – that an elaborate and pervasive mythology surrounds the subject. Even experienced officers readily subscribe to this mythology and indeed seek to perpetuate it. Such is the potency of the police culture at certain stations that arguments which would seem confounded by daily experience in the interview room are nevertheless presented as self-evident truths. Although there are variations from officer to officer and from station to station in the extent to which such views are held, it is apparent that the problems created for interviewers by the exercise of the right to silence and the extent to which these problems are exacerbated by obstructive solicitors are greatly exaggerated by many police officers.

The author was himself told on many occasions by police officers how certain firms of solicitors operate a blanket policy of advising suspects to say nothing to interviewers, quite regardless of the circumstances of the case or the situation of the individual suspect. Despite the author's requests for the relevant firms to be named, no officer ever identified a single lawyer who routinely advised suspects to remain silent. The insistence that such firms exist remains unshaken, however, and there seems almost no way to explode the surrounding folklore. Legal advisers are seen by a majority of officers as threatening elements in an interview, consistently advising clients to answer no questions at all.[28] Lawyers on the other hand tend to see themselves, if it is not putting it too euphemistically, as on the side of "justice", anxious to protect the innocent but happy to see the majority of their clients, whom they regard as guilty, receiving their just deserts.

Lawyers' views on video taped interviews

While the lawyers who attend interviews at police stations have in general greeted the advent of tape recording procedures with great enthusiasm, it

---

[28] On other aspects of the mythology, see J. Baldwin (1992).

is strange that they do not seem to be playing the tapes with much frequency. In the author's study, only 69 (11.5 per cent) of the audio tapes were requested by defence lawyers. Even less use was made of the video tapes, with under three per cent being requested. Although such figures have to be treated with caution because lawyers are not involved in all cases, they do nonetheless indicate that lawyers are very selective in the extent to which they are prepared to listen to tapes. It seems common practice for lawyers to confine their requests to those cases in which a not guilty plea is anticipated, and many are unwilling to play the tapes in other circumstances. This seems to apply regardless of whether they attended the original interview.

The reluctance of lawyers to request tapes is curious since each of the police forces included in the present study supplied audio tapes free of charge on request.[29] There is certainly a good deal more circumspection amongst solicitors about the value of video tape than about audio tape, though it has only been at the Edmonton station that solicitors have advised their clients in any numbers not to allow interviews to be video recorded. In figures made available to the author by the Metropolitan Police,[30] it is apparent that there has been a growing disinclination on the part of solicitors to have interviews video recorded over the period in which the video experiments have been conducted. In the early days of the experiment at the Edmonton station, about ninety per cent of the first batch of suspects agreed to be interviewed on video, a proportion that fell to eighty per cent in late 1991 and early 1992. About three quarters of suspects who declined did so after having received legal advice, and the latest figures indicate that only about seventy per cent of all interviews in which lawyers were present were being video recorded at Edmonton.

Thus, while most interviews (even at Edmonton) continue to be video recorded, there is a significant minority of cases in which the defence is objecting to it. This disinclination does not, however, apparently represent any concerted opposition to the video taping procedures on the part of lawyers. Although a few solicitors advise their clients not to have their interviews on video, it is more common for them to exercise a

---

[29] Where solicitors request a copy of a video taped interview in the West Midlands and West Mercia, they are required to supply the appropriate number of blank tapes. The tapes have then to be sent away for copying and this can sometimes take up to ten days. Many solicitors, when informed of this procedure, withdraw their request and settle for a copy of the audio tape which can as a rule be supplied within 24 hours. In Edmonton, where three recordings are made simultaneously at the time of the interview, this problem does not arise, and video recordings can be supplied immediately to solicitors.

[30] The author is indebted to Detective Inspector Slade and Inspector Johnson of the Metropolitan Police for supplying these figures.

judgment on a case by case basis as to when video recording is in the interests of their clients and when it is not.

Solicitors' lukewarm attitudes towards the introduction of video recordings were apparent in interviews conducted with them. Interviews were carried out with representatives of the six main law firms who most regularly attended the police stations in Birmingham, Wolverhampton, Redditch and Edmonton at which video recording facilities had been introduced.[31] A response rate of 83 per cent was obtained, with four firms declining to take part.[32] An attempt was made to explore with legal representatives a number of issues, including the way they saw their role when they attended interviews at police stations, their relations with the police, and their views on the video experiments. These lawyers were well placed to comment on such matters since most of them were busy practitioners whose firms did a good deal of criminal work. Three quarters of them said that they attended interviews at police stations at least twice a week and a quarter as many as five interviews a week.

Most lawyers said that they enjoyed good relations with the police. Over half described their relations as "very good" or "excellent" and only two of them said that they were "poor." Times have, it seems, changed and lawyers have come to expect a better reception at police stations than they encountered in the pre-P.A.CE. era. Police officers have themselves accepted the presence of solicitors at interviews with a greater equanimity than would have been the case a decade ago. Only two solicitors interviewed in this study reported that they nowadays experience resistance or hostility from the police when attending at interviews. Lawyers tend to make an effort to maintain these relations and avoid being seen to rock to boat. There is nonetheless an implicit assumption (as in the following quote from an interview with a solicitor in Wolverhampton) that mutual respect has to be earned:

"I haven't encountered any problems at all during the time I've been doing interviews, but I think it's how you approach the police and how you approach the job. A lot of them suspect that you've told your client not to say anything but it's not the case. There have been occasions when my clients have said nothing when I've felt that I've had to tell the police that I had not advised them to make 'no comment'. I've felt I've had to do that to maintain my credibility with the police."

---

[31] The firms that were contacted were those that most frequently attended interviews (whether video recorded or not) in each area.
[32] One firm in Birmingham, one in Wolverhampton and two in London declined to participate in the study.

There is an unwritten understanding that, if they are to preserve good working relations with the police, then there has to be a certain amount of give-and-take on both sides. A solicitor in Redditch summed up well the view held by many of those interviewed:

"I suppose it's down to personalities. I imagine there may be some solicitors who are a bit more brittle than I am. I'm a fairly compliant sort of personality because I find it easier to toe the line of least resistance. I think I can achieve more in that way than by coming up hard against the police. Maybe our bonhomie is a bit artificial but I think it's better to do it that way rather than trying to be antagonistic and it's easier to achieve a much better result. I don't know what they are really thinking, but on the surface we get along very well."

As already noted, there was less enthusiasm about the use of video equipment amongst lawyers than amongst the police officers whose views had also been canvassed on the subject. Whereas 86 per cent of police officers were favourably disposed towards the use of video (many enthusiastically so), just under a half of the legal representatives spoke in such terms. It is nonetheless fair to describe most of the lawyers as being mildly favourable or ambivalent about it, and there were only three who were so strongly opposed that they advised their clients not to consent to their interviews being recorded on video. It is worth citing extracts from the interview material to illustrate the nature of the lawyers' main misgivings:

Interview 2 (Birmingham) "It's easy for somebody who is intelligent and articulate to speak in front of a camera, but, if you take the average punter, he knows that, when he is on camera, it may be in effect before an audience of a hundred people afterwards. It is then very nerve-racking to answer questions. It's like being on T.V., bombarded with questions. It may be that, because of sheer nerves, a client may not perform well in an interview. It puts extra pressure on them. Unfortunately people show the same signs of lying because of the pressure they're under because a video is running. Being nervous can be misinterpreted, simply because it is being video recorded. I would never agree to another interview being videoed because I do think it puts undue pressure on the defendant. My job is not to secure a conviction but to protect that person in that police station at that time."

Interview 3 (Birmingham) "I can't see immediately any advantage in having that medium. It may well have some disadvantages. Clients might look a bit blasé or a bit arrogant or whatever. Unless he's openly expressing remorse, I can't see any advantage for the client. I would advise clients not to go on video because it may be detrimental to them. I can't see any advantages, so I would say, 'Play safe. What's the point if it's not going to do you any good?'"

Interview 4 (Wolverhampton) "I dare say there's a good side but I don't know what it is. To be honest, I don't see there's any point in it. I don't see it as a desirable innovation although I don't really have any reservations about it. I just don't think there's any point in spending the money on equipment, to be truthful. I don't think a video recording is going to do any more than the audio tape would do anyway."

Interview 1 (Redditch) "As far as I have been involved, it has been very much a waste of time. I would have thought that, with a tape recording and a solicitor present, there is no necessity for it in anything less than a serious arrestable offence. I regard tape recordings as being vital, but I don't see that videos add anything to tape recordings."

Interview 3 (Redditch) "I can't see the point of it. I'm not interested in what my clients look like. I have no strong view about the video experiments. At the moment I cannot think there's any need for them because the audio tape is more than adequate. I'm interested in what the man has said, not how he is sitting, or whether he is scratching his ear. 'Reservations' is too strong a word. I wouldn't say I've got reservations about the video. That's too positive a thought! At the moment I just can't see the need for it. My feeling is that it's a bit of a waste of money."

Interview 4 (Redditch) "It's very difficult to see what the benefit of video recording interviews is. I would have thought that the audio is perfectly adequate. I've no reservations as such. I'm just slightly bemused as to what purpose it serves."

Interview 5 (Edmonton) "I am completely against it and always advise my clients not to be videod. The reason for this is that I think it's an artificial situation. The suspect is under considerable pressure and will not secure any advantage by having himself filmed. The whole point of videos, as I understand it, is that he is being seen as he normally is. So I always advise against and I think the audio tape provides the necessary safeguards."

Interview 6 (Edmonton) "I don't think that it helps many of my clients to be video recorded although overall I think it's a good idea. I'm not entirely convinced that it's in all my clients' best interests all the time. Everyone has something to worry about, something to hide in an interview and obviously they are not their true selves. There is some sort of nervousness about them which can come over in their voices. They can come over in terms of biting their nails, a nervous tic on their faces, and I think juries may misconstrue that. Sometimes, with somebody kept in a cell for a few hours, they don't look themselves. They haven't got a shirt and tie; they don't look smart because of the facilities. So really you are not seeing the client as I would like you to see the client. You see a different person from the real person and that applies to everyone in video recordings."

Only a small minority of the lawyers were firmly opposed to the video recording of interviews: many more were apathetic or ambivalent, seeing it as adding little, if anything, to audio recording and in that sense a waste of scarce resources. There is some justification for this view, and the benefits of video recordings tend often to be overstated. Police officers when interviewed commonly made extravagant claims about the importance of observing suspects' body language on the video,[33] whereas the tapes have little to offer in this respect. It is likely that significant benefits will be identified in only a small minority of all cases in which video equipment is used,[34] and the interviews conducted with legal representatives in this study tended to confirm this.

Notwithstanding the signal lack of enthusiasm amongst lawyers for the video recording of police interviews, it is something of an exaggeration to suggest that opposition from the legal profession would represent a serious obstacle to its introduction if that were deemed the appropriate course. All of the solicitors who were interviewed in this study recognised the value of the tape recording of interviews, and several of them favoured the introduction of video recorders, albeit without much enthusiasm. The author's reading of the situation is that most lawyers are waiting to be convinced.

Lawyers' attitude to their role at interviews

One major advantage of being able to talk to legal representatives about the video experiments was that it provided an opportunity to explore with them their own role at interviews. What did they perceive to be their appropriate function? To what extent did they see themselves (as police officers commonly view them) as obstructive, even subversive? How did

---

[33] The application of the concept of "body language" to police interviewing has now spawned a massive and complex psychological literature. A careful reading of this literature indicates, however, that the subject cannot be regarded as more than pseudo-science (or "psychobabble" as it is sometimes seen). At best the notion of body language provides an uncertain basis upon which to draw inferences of truthfulness, credibility, guilt or whatever; at worst it can be dangerous in that worthless and misleading conclusions may be drawn. Signals tend to be interpreted by police officers in self-confirmatory ways, with guilt inferred from suspects whether they respond with calmness or hyper-activity, silence or loquaciousness. The complex psychological literature is well summarised in M. Argyle (1988).
[34] The main benefits of having interviews recorded on video are discussed in J. Baldwin (1992) at pp. 6–8.

they square any pretensions to be "adversarial" with their own rather passive performance on tape? It has already been seen that few legal representatives considered it worthwhile, other than in exceptional circumstances, to engage in confrontation with police interviewers. How, then, do they see their function if they are not the adversaries of the police?

No fewer than 85 per cent of the lawyers contacted in this study saw their role as being confined to two central functions, first to advise their clients as to their position before questioning commenced, and, secondly, to act as a referee in the interview to ensure that fair play was observed.[35] They said that they found little to complain about in the way that most interviews were conducted, and they therefore saw little need for any interventions. They emphatically did not see it as their overriding obligation to secure the acquittal of clients whom they believed to be guilty. As one solicitor in Redditch put it:

> "I'm primarily there to help and advise the suspect but also (and here I think I speak for all the solicitors in Redditch) we are a bridge between the suspect and the police because of this relationship we've built up with the police. You are there partly as a communicator between two opposing factions. I don't see it as part of my job (and this is a personal opinion and it might mean that I'm not a good solicitor) to help people evade the consequences of their actions. I am there to make sure that in that situation they are treated properly, that the Codes of Practice are complied with and generally do what I can to help them. I don't think there's a single solicitor in Redditch who would encourage a suspect to tell lies or mislead the police in order to avoid the consequences of what he's done. Where a suspect wishes to stay silent, I make it very clear to them that they have that right and that it is up to the prosecution to prove the allegation against them. I regard that as one of my basic functions. But you've got to encourage people to admit that they've done something to avoid them messing everyone around and wasting everybody's time. It is in my view sensible to advise a client that, if it's true that he had nothing to hide, that he's done nothing wrong, then there's no reason why he should not cooperate with the police in the interview."

While it would not be accurate to say that most lawyers describe their role as being to facilitate police questioning, they certainly do not see it in the opposite terms. Most lawyers view themselves more as neutral referees, ready to intervene without hesitation if questioning gets out of

---

[35] The Law Society states that the purpose of a solicitor's presence is to advise the suspect, to ensure that the interview is being fairly conducted, to assist communication between the suspect and interviewer, and to protect the suspect's welfare. (Law Society, 1988 at para. 9.3).

hand, rather than assuming an adversary stance from the outset. This is how some of the lawyers themselves described their role in interviews:

Interview 3 (Birmingham) "I don't think it's my function under the revised Codes to stop a client who wants to confess. Some solicitors can do that and it's not classed as hindering the police. But my view is that I've explained everything to him, and, if he wants to come clean and confess it, I'm not going to stand there and say that he shouldn't confess. It's his choice at the end of the day. It's just the same when clients who decide to go 'no comment' (or we advise to go 'no comment') start talking to them. Now I don't think it's my function then to say, 'Well hang on a minute, shut up, we've decided to go no comment,' if he's decided to answer the questions that are put to him. He's been cautioned, he's had advice."

Interview 5 (Birmingham) "Providing the officers act within the rules, then there is not a great deal that you can say. You've got to be careful that you're not priming or guiding the client. At the end of the day, there is perhaps some responsibility to justice, but our prime responsibility is to the client."

Interview 6 (Birmingham) "I see the role of solicitor at an interview as being to obtain as much information from the police officers as possible as to the nature of the case, the arrest and what evidence they have. Then you can advise the client about what course of action they should take. Once the interview starts, my responsibility is to interfere if either the questions are manifestly unfair or if I think that perhaps the police are bullying, hectoring or attempting to cross-examine a suspect who has given an explanation which is all they are entitled to. But I don't see it as being my role to say, 'You shouldn't answer that' unless it is an improper question. The decision to answer a question is the suspect's, and, as long as he'd been properly advised as to his rights and the choices he can make, it's up to him. As time goes by, I find that the need to interrupt an interview has become less."

Interview 2 (Wolverhampton) "In the majority of interviews, all the police stick to P.A.C.E. Sometimes they can get a little bit aggressive if the client is telling lies. I tell my clients before the interview that, if they start to feel uncomfortable, they must request a break and a consultation with me. The only time I speak during an interview is when they are introducing everyone who's in the room. That is the only time that I take part in an interview until maybe at the end when I am asked if there is anything I would like to add, and it's very rare that I have to make a comment. So during the interview, there is no active part."

Interview 6 (Wolverhampton) "The classic advice of days gone by was to tell one's clients to say nothing. I think those days have gone. Nowadays I participate in interviews as little as possible because I feel that, if a solicitor interrupts too much, then it starts to become his interview and you've got to bear in mind what it will sound like in court. But it's rarely necessary to interrupt an interview. The very fact that we're there generally influences police officers to behave themselves."

Interview 1 (Redditch) "You don't want to be in a position where a client is overawed by the police. On the other hand we are not there to impede the investigation. I take it that my role is to make sure that the rules are obeyed, that the client isn't brow-beaten and that he isn't asked to answer questions that he can't understand. Within those limits, I tend not to interfere. We are not allowed, as I see it, to interpose ourselves between the police and the client in a way that would seem to suggest that we are batting for our clients."

Interview 6 (Redditch) "I generally wouldn't intervene in an interview because, by then, I've had my turn and the client has had all the advice they wanted. Once the police take over, that's it. I'll just sit there. But if the police start asking questions that are difficult to answer (three questions wrapped in one or things like that), I'll disentangle the question if the client is having difficulty understanding it or else omits an important part of what he has already told me or fails to do himself sufficient credit. But once we are in the interview, I am not going to say someone, 'Don't answer that question' because the police have taken over at that stage. I wouldn't intervene very often in an interview. My role would be a passive one. I would only intervene when the interviewing becomes harsh or oppressive, but that would only arise in the odd case. You will have observed on the videos how solicitors sit quietly in the corner."

Interview 3 (Edmonton) "When we attend at the station, we ask the police officer for a broad outline of what the case is about. We discuss that with the client in private. If he had anything in particular that he wants to say to us, he can do so. Then we advise him on how to proceed with the interview. Once the interview proper starts, I personally don't get too involved. I take the view that it's the client's interview. I would fully explain to the client before we begin that, if he's not sure about anything or feels he is being pressured, he can stop the interview and he has a right to ask for a private consultation. But I tend not take an active role in the interview unless I think that things are very much getting out of hand. But that doesn't happen very often."

It is obvious from these quotes that lawyers do not see themselves in the way that many police officers portray them. Their common posture in interviews at police stations is conciliatory and acquiescent. This is how they describe themselves, and it is not wishful thinking or a desire to pull the wool over the researcher's eyes: it squares with lawyers' behaviour at the interviews themselves.

Conclusion

As noted earlier in this report, a critical question is whether lawyers should be acting more forcefully on their clients' behalf at the police station. There is a good deal of scope for them to do so, and there were only a few lawyers on the video tapes who demonstrated that they could wield much authority in the interview room if the need arose. Some lawyers were more tolerant than were others of police officers who adopted harrying tactics, who persisted doggedly with certain lines of questioning or who made crude assumptions of guilt.[36] Searching questions need to be asked, therefore, about how far legal representatives – who are in most instances unqualified legal personnel – can be said to be providing adequate protection to their clients in the police station.

The lawyers' view of their role at police interviews reflects the way that their attitudes have been moulded by the history of their relations with the police. The interview takes place on police territory and it is police officers who are in charge of it. Officers often describe it as "their" interview, and the lawyers contacted in this study did not commonly see it in other terms. Although police attitudes towards the presence of solicitors have shifted in the course of the past decade – reflecting to a considerable extent the changes brought in by the P.A.C.E. legislation – lawyers continue to be treated with circumspection and suspicion. While they are no longer regarded as gatecrashers at interviews, they are nonetheless only tolerated at police stations if they behave appropriately. Advising clients not to answer questions or intervening at interviews are not seen by police as reasonable forms of behaviour. It is only if they toe the line that lawyers are regarded as acceptable participants at police interviews.

Passivity and compliance on the part of lawyers are therefore the normal, the expected, almost the required responses at the police station. Solicitors are conditioned by their history, their experience, even their own professional training and guidance, to be passive in the police interview room, and the existing rules reinforce this by giving police officers the upper hand. The lawyers' role in the interview room remains a precarious one, and it is no real surprise to note that the junior staff who mainly turn up to police stations are more inclined to facilitate police questioning than they are to challenge it.

---

[36] As noted earlier, it is important to bear in mind, when assessing the role of legal representatives, that a majority of police interviews on tape are low key affairs, whether lawyers are present or not : see further J. Baldwin (1992) pp. 12–18.

SUPERVISION OF POLICE INVESTIGATIONS IN SERIOUS CRIMINAL CASES

JOHN BALDWIN AND TIMOTHY MOLONEY

Background to the Study

It is extraordinary that so little is known about the way that police enquiries in serious criminal cases are conducted. There has been a considerable amount of research which has explored the question of detection – largely exploding the myth that this is done by means of lengthy, painstaking enquiries – but little effort has been expended in finding out how major investigations are run and how they are supervised. This lack of information is to be regretted, since it is now widely acknowledged that the miscarriages of justice that have occurred in the recent past might have been avoided had the early stages in the police investigations been more professionally conducted and had greater efforts been made by senior officers to ensure that proper procedures were followed.

When one examines the available research evidence, it is clear that police investigations rarely conform to the popular image of the detective solving crimes by tenacity and ingenuity. Indeed, the myth of investigative policing belies an altogether more mundane reality: most police work is reactive rather than proactive;[1] most crimes are only solved if members of the public are able to supply information to the police about the identity of the offender,[2] and the investigators' task is less concerned with crime detection than with assembling the prosecution case in order to satisfy the relevant authorities that prosecution and conviction are justified.[3]

This evidence suggests, then, that investigations tend to be straightforward and short. If no one is arrested within a few hours of the offence being reported to the police, then it is unlikely that the investigation will be continued for very long. Special investigative techniques, for example those involving forensic skills, are only infrequently employed, and the conclusion drawn in the United States that "somewhere around 97 percent of cleared crimes will be cleared no

---

[1] Police investigations are characterised as "reactive" where members of the public are responsible for bringing offences to the attention of the police, and as "proactive" where the police act on their own initiative: see A.J. Reiss (1971) at pp 63–65. There is a considerable amount of empirical evidence from research conducted in this country which demonstrates that police investigations are largely "reactive" in character: see in particular A.K. Bottomley and C. Coleman (1976); M. Zander (1979); R. Mawby (1979), and D. Steer (1980).
[2] As one writer has put it, "the police are able to solve a crime if someone tells them who committed it; if no one tells them, it is unlikely they will make an arrest" (C.E. Silberman, 1978, at p.218).
[3] A somewhat different picture emerges in relation to the investigation and detection of non-indictable offences: see R. Mawby (1979) chapter 1.

matter what the investigators do, as long as the obvious routine follow-up steps are taken"[4] probably applies just as much in this country. This indicates that there is unlikely to be in most investigations a strong relationship between the amount of effort expended by police officers and the probability of detection.

The routine nature of much case processing might suggest that there is little room for supervision – and perhaps little need for it either. Yet even though police officers may play only a limited part in solving crime, their role in collecting the evidence in the case to support prosecution is of great significance and is by no means routine. It requires, for example, that witnesses and suspects be interviewed fairly and in accordance with the relevant regulations; evidence has to be collected systematically, and set procedures adhered to. Things can go badly wrong and miscarriages of justice can occur when these stages of an investigation are poorly conducted or inadequately supervised. And we should not overlook the fact that there remains a minority of investigations, involving specialist departments such as the Regional Crime Squad, in which there is a need for painstaking enquiries, forensic skills and the like if a case is to be cleared.[5]

An attempt was made in the present study to examine the way that police investigations of serious offences were supervised. It was not possible, given the constraints of time, to select a representative group of such cases, and a sample of 45 serious incidents, drawn from four hundred cases that had been examined in an earlier evaluation of video taping experiments, was used.[6] In that study, a hundred interviews from each of four police stations (the Belgrave Road and Wednesfield stations in the West Midlands, Redditch in West Mercia and Edmonton in the Metropolitan Police District) had been examined. The 45 cases included in the present study involved 74 suspects whose interviews had been video recorded,[7] and the

---

[4] P.W. Greenwood, J.M. Chaiken and J. Petersilia (1977) at p.227.
[5] It is, however, important to note that, even in the small proportion of cases in which forensic skills are used, their role is likely to be as confirmation of suspicions already formed rather than as a key part of detection. M. Ramsay (1987) notes, in relation to the work of the Forensic Science Service:
> Cases where a suspect had been identified at the time of referral accounted for a high proportion of the total (79 per cent). The F.S.S. were not asked to reveal whodunnit but to corroborate suspicions already well formed. (p.12).

[6] The first part of this evaluation, which started in the West Midlands in 1989, was funded by the Leverhulme Trust, and further funding was subsequently provided by the Home Office to enable the study to be extended to other areas.
[7] There were a number of other suspects, whose interviews were not video recorded, involved in these investigations. Large numbers of suspects were, for example, interviewed in one extensive murder enquiry in London, only two of whom featured in the video samples.

investigations were selected because they represented the most serious offences in the sample of video taped interviews. They did not therefore constitute a scientifically selected sample but included all murders and other serious violence, major robberies, professionally organised and executed criminal activities, arson and other offences of comparable gravity. Seventeen of the 45 cases were handled by officers in Birmingham, eleven in Wednesfield, eight in Redditch and nine in Edmonton.[8] Table 1 presents details of the offences which made up the sample.

Table 1: Types of offences included in the study

		%
(Attempted) murder	4	8.9
Other serious violence	6	13.3
Rape	2	4.5
Robbery	14	31.1
Arson	6	13.3
Drugs dealing	4	8.9
Organised burglary	6	13.3
Kidnapping	3	6.7
	45	100.0

The tight deadline set by the Royal Commission – the project commenced in September 1991 and had to be completed by the end of March 1992 – meant that it was not possible to undertake the study in a way that might satisfy the purists. We had no time, for instance, to examine major investigations from scratch or even to observe supervisory officers at work. We had to content ourselves instead with interviewing the police officers who had been put in charge of the 45 enquiries. Since it takes more than a year for many cases (especially those of a serious nature) to be dealt with by the courts from the initial reporting of the crime, it was obvious that, if we had attempted to follow enquiries from their inception, we could have done no more in the time available than observe the early stages, and then only in a small number of cases.

The study that we carried out is therefore subject to a number of weaknesses. It is concerned with only a relatively small number of police investigations and the information on these cases comes largely from the police. Furthermore, the sample consists only of investigations that were successful to the extent that at least one suspect had at some stage been brought to the station for questioning. We know nothing of those

---

[8] There appeared to be variations from station to station in the way that investigations were conducted, but, given the relatively small number of cases at individual stations, it was not thought worthwhile to draw conclusions about such variations in this report.

investigations which proved entirely fruitless and which might have been dropped by the police prematurely, belatedly or in any other circumstances.

Although this was not a random group of police enquiries into serious cases, there were nonetheless certain important gains that we derived, albeit largely fortuitously, from studying investigations in the manner adopted in this study. First, a good deal was already known about all the cases from playing the video recording of the suspects' interviews and from talking to officers about the video experiments. We could be confident in selecting cases for inclusion in the sample that the offences themselves were not of a minor or technical nature (as is, for example, the case with many robberies). Secondly, an assessment had already been made of the way that the interviews had been conducted with the suspects concerned, and, since it had been estimated that almost forty per cent of them had been carried out less than satisfactorily,[9] supervisors could be tackled in this study about how this was allowed to happen and how they saw their own role in the questioning of suspects. Finally, all of the cases had been tracked through the criminal process so that, by the time that this study commenced, it was known whether cases had got off the ground, which suspects had been prosecuted and with what result.

These proved considerable benefits and meant that, when we interviewed officers about the way they had supervised investigations, we were in a position to talk to them in a somewhat more challenging manner than would have been the case had the investigations still been running. It is also worth stressing that, whatever anxieties we might have had about the methods we were obliged to adopt in the study, these were largely dispelled when we confronted the officers concerned. We were struck – occasionally taken aback – by their disarming frankness and were satisfied that, in the great majority of cases, the officers had given their accounts of the investigations without seeking to obscure the way things had been done. All officers allowed us to tape record the interviews we conducted with them, and the extensive use we make in this report of the materials derived from these interviews will serve to underline the officers' commendable candour.

Since the video recordings of the interviews with suspects included in this study had been made in 1989 and 1990, it was not perhaps surprising that, when we sought interviews with supervising officers late in 1991, certain difficulties were encountered in locating them. Many officers had changed stations, others were away on courses and one had retired. It required a great deal of perseverance to find the relevant officers. In the event, we were successful in interviewing 41 of the 45

---

[9] See J. Baldwin (1992) for discussion of how these assessments were made.

officers (91 per cent), and only one actually declined. Officers were contacted at all hours of the day and night, and it is appropriate that we acknowledge here our sincere gratitude to all those who participated in the study for the generous assistance they gave us. [10]

Time had not, as we had feared, dimmed the memories of the officers, and there was only one who experienced serious difficulties in recalling details of the case in which we were interested. Talking to these officers confirmed the fact that the vast majority of the offences were of a serious nature. 72 per cent of the investigations had resulted in prosecution, and no fewer than 86 per cent of those against whom charges were brought and who were subsequently convicted at court received custodial sentences (two of which were suspended).[11]

The notion of "supervision"

Textbooks on research methods warn researchers about making assumptions which will pre-determine the results of an enquiry, and it became clear from the very first interview that we conducted that officers were uncertain and uneasy about our use of the word "supervision" to describe their role. Officers repeatedly went out of their way to coin alternative descriptions of what their role entailed. These alternatives suggest an important phenomenon: other than the few high-ranking officers leading major teams of investigators, police officers on the whole shy away from seeing themselves as supervisors, preferring instead to regard supervision in terms of "teamwork" or "partnership" or "coordination" or simply as a "joint venture." Although in this report we shall describe the officers in charge of cases as "supervisors", it is nonetheless important to recognise that this is our description and is not necessarily the one that the officers themselves would accept as appropriate.

One main reason why officers are reluctant to see themselves as supervisors is that it is often officers of constable rank who are the supervisors, even in serious cases. Given the gravity of the incidents involved, it was surprising to note how junior many supervisors were. Only nine of them (20 per cent) were of inspector rank or higher, fourteen (31 per cent) were sergeants, and 22 (49 per cent) were of constable rank, including four police constables. Few of the cases that we examined were ones in which special squads were formed, large numbers of officers drafted in or incident rooms set up. Indeed, as the following table shows,

---

[10] We are also grateful for the assistance that was offered to us at all stations both in identifying the supervisors concerned in each case and in ascertaining their whereabouts at the time this study was undertaken.

[11] 62 per cent of those who were sentenced to imprisonment received terms in excess of two years (including two life sentences).

only 22 per cent of enquiries involved more than ten officers and over sixty per cent four or fewer.

Table 2: Number of officers involved in the enquiries

		%
A sole officer	2	4.9
2 officers	13	31.7
3–4 officers	11	26.8
5–10 officers	6	14.6
11–20 officers	3	7.3
21–50 officers	2	4.9
Over 50 officers	4	9.8
Not known	4	-
	45	100.0

It was apparent, even in the very early stages of the study, that few officers viewed themselves as genuine supervisors. More importantly, few actually sought to play that kind of role. In most cases, officers said that they were members of a small team of equals, working on a much more democratic basis than the term "supervision" implied. This is how one detective constable in Birmingham expressed his reservations to us about the use of the word "supervision":[12]

Case 9 (Birmingham) "The way we worked at Belgrave Road was, although I was the officer in charge of the case, it wasn't really a supervisory situation: it was just me and my partner dealing with it. It wasn't a supervisor/subordinate situation. We didn't work like that. It was just a matter of us combining our efforts and sorting out the interview together. The officer in charge of the case does the case papers. That effectively is the end of the officer's involvement, unless the defendant then pleads not guilty in court. The officer would then in effect take charge of the case on the day of the court appearance and liaise with the others in the case. But I think your word 'supervision' is the wrong word. I think it would be better to say 'director of enquiries' or 'coordinator' if you like. It's only a nominal role as a D.C. It's not a supervisory role, though it worked well enough."

The word, "supervision", was not much liked, then, by the officers to whom we spoke, and it is a concept that is very much in the eye of the beholder in the sense that it is left largely to the individual officer to decide how he or she will play the role. As the officer in the quote above

---

[12] In some of the quotes from interviews, minor details have been altered so as to preserve the anonymity of officers and suspects.

observed, it is no more than a nominal activity in very many cases. It was clear from the interviews we conducted that most officers in charge of enquiries do not view it as their business to direct operations, to tell others what to do or to criticise them.[13] They tend to see it not only as unnecessary but even demeaning to peers or subordinates for them to be concerned to any extent in their activities, let alone to comment upon them. Even when officers in charge of enquiries were asked whether they would offer "advice" to other officers working on a case, they were still hesitant to see their role in this light. They preferred to talk instead about "discussion" amongst the members of a small team. One officer leading an enquiry into an attempted murder summarised this viewpoint as follows:

Case 11 (Birmingham) "There were a number of officers who were working on the case (including a Scenes of Crimes team), but there were really only three of us working together as a team. We were more of a self-advisory group. We would say to each other, 'How are we going to do this?' We tossed it about in the office and someone would come up with a good idea. So I don't think that 'advice' is the right word to use. Although I was the officer in charge of the case, since we were a close-knit team, it was very much a combined effort and the other officers would hardly think of me as being in charge. It's a nominal thing. It's just that someone's name is on the file. At the end of the day, it's only if it's one of those cases where you have to decide whether you are going to do something or not (charge, caution, bail or whatever) that that would be left to the officer in charge. Even then, nine times out of ten, it would be an obvious decision. In this case, it was really a coordination of efforts although there were quite a lot of resources to coordinate. It was a supervisor's job in effect but it was made easy by the fact that we were a good team working on it together."

It appears to be only in the large-scale investigations, involving teams of officers with a senior officer in charge, that supervision assumes real rather than merely formal significance. There were ten cases of this kind in the sample, and these included murders, arson, rape and two professionally executed burglaries. In these investigations, supervision was far more comprehensive. A single officer of inspector rank or higher assumed substantive responsibility for directing operations involving a sizeable group of officers. These senior officers gave orders, checked on progress, coordinated tactics and held regular briefings. In all the other cases, things were much more fluid, more informal and more democratic.

---

[13] Not interfering in other officers' work forms a maxim of the "Cop's Code" described in a study of police work in New York City conducted by E. Reuss-Ianni and F.A.J. Ianni (1963). See also Kaye (1991).

Enquiries in the latter type of case were typically conducted at divisional or subdivisional level, involving local crime with victims and offenders often living in the same vicinity. Detectives were fond of talking about their "patch" as an area with which they felt some familiarity and affinity. They were not therefore for the most part the sort of cases that required lengthy investigations. If offenders were to be brought to book at all, they needed to be arrested quickly. The following are a few typical quotes from supervisory officers (only three of whom were above the rank of constable) describing the way they saw their role in such enquiries. It is interesting to note again their reticence in viewing themselves as genuine supervisors:

Case 1 (Birmingham) "That particular case was the same as a lot of them. You get a piece of paper on your desk saying, 'A robbery has occurred, this is the man who was robbed, this is what he says has happened.' The first thing to do is to find out if he will identify someone, and in that case the man thought he would. So we took him to look at some photographs up the town and he picked him out. I don't think it's a matter of being supervised on a job like that or supervising others. It's not supervision as such; it's a job where everybody goes and does it together. O.K., someone's name has to go on the paperwork to say they're the officer in charge of the case. But most of the time on the C.I.D., everything is done as a team rather than one person saying, 'You do that and you do the other.'"

Case 7 (Birmingham) "It wasn't a question of leading an enquiry; it was just a question of making sure that the case [a serious assault] was handled well. You've mentioned two or three times 'supervising the enquiry.' I wouldn't really put it that way My role was to get the evidence together, collate it, do the interviews and prepare the case for the Crown Court. I wouldn't use the word 'supervision.'"

Case 22 (Wolverhampton) "It's difficult to talk about supervision really because the other officers involved were Detective Constables, and I don't think that I 'supervised' them. My role isn't like that of the superintendent in a murder enquiry. It's only when something really needs to be sorted out that the supervisor in a case like this is of any importance. These cases are more or less straightforward. You don't need anyone to say, 'You'll do this; you'll do that.' The people I was working with at that stage are experienced people. They should know what they're doing so it's not necessary for me to give orders. You make suggestions. It all depends on how you put yourself over."

Case 23 (Wolverhampton) "I was working with a Detective Sergeant, and, whilst I suppose I was in charge of the case because my name was on the file, in reality we were working together. My role was just to prepare the file."

Case 27 (Wolverhampton) "I didn't offer the other officer any advice because we've worked together for a number of years so we know what's required. At the end of the day, somebody's name has got to go on the paperwork. If it's not me, it's my partner. You both have joint responsibility. If we deal with a case, we don't squabble about who's going to be O.I.C. [officer in charge], we get on with it and my role in the case was interviewing, putting together a file, getting it to court, getting him remanded. That's basically it."

Case 31 (Redditch) "Obviously, supervision-wise, it's a question of deciding who's going to interview the prisoner, then de-briefing after the interview and deciding what charges to prefer. It was just a straightforward case [of robbery]."

Case 33 (Redditch) "It was a typical case of arson. It was a bread-and-butter case dealt with as a matter of course. I didn't think twice about it. It was a clearcut case. We could see what path to take; it was a nice, steady, straight-down-the-line process, everything fell into place. There were no complications at all, albeit a very serious situation in the first place."

Case 39 (London) "It was a straightforward smash-and-grab. There was no need for me to give the other officers any advice. The blokes who were working with this job were men of about ten or thirteen years' service and there's no way I'm going to start teaching them to suck eggs. There was nothing to it."

Case 45 (London) "You don't even think that you're supervising in a case like this. You know that certain things have to be done, that they have to be done correctly and you make sure that they are. It comes as second nature to you. I'm aware that the case has to be supervised and that it is my job to do it properly, but you don't physically think to yourself, 'Right, I must go now and supervise', because I've been in the police service a long time and the role of supervision is almost second nature to me. Although it was a rape case, it was a simple, straightforward, bread-and-butter type of case. Even if I don't necessarily consciously think that I must 'supervise' in a case, I do think, 'This needs to be done, let's do it'. But it is a team effort. There's not a great deal of supervision that needs to be done in this kind of case because I'm wearing two hats, one as the investigator, the other as the supervisor."

As is apparent in several of these quotes from interviews with supervising police officers, many of the investigations appeared to be treated on a routine basis, and one could not fail to be struck in interviewing the officers by the nonchalant, almost casual, approach that they commonly adopted. It was not, however, our impression that the officers did not care about the outcome of the enquiries they were conducting. Their nonchalance stemmed more from self-confidence – almost all felt that they could handle the investigation without difficulty – and this is in part a reflection of their dependability and reliance upon the immediate colleagues with whom they worked. "I've never worked with a lazy C.I.D. officer or anyone I've had problems with" is how one officer in Birmingham expressed it to us.

As a separate part of the study, we contacted Chief Crown Prosecutors in each of the three areas to see whether the Crown Prosecution Service had been involved at the investigative stage in the cases included in the samples or had made suggestions to the police about the way any of the investigations were handled. It was obvious from the details we were given that the involvement of the Crown Prosecution Service was minimal at most. The information could not be supplied in all of the cases in which we were interested, but everything we were given pointed clearly to the conclusion that the contribution of Crown Prosecutors was restricted to the offering of advice about the appropriate charges on only a few occasions. They were not involved in any enquiry at the investigative stage, nor were they asked to comment on whether any suspect should or should not be charged.

The information provided by Chief Crown Prosecutors confirmed the picture that had been presented by the police officers interviewed about these investigations. Despite the relative gravity of the offences in question, the investigations were for the most part viewed as straightforward, unproblematic and satisfactorily conducted by the officers concerned. There was not a single case in which Crown Prosecutors had requested that further information be collected or had criticisms of the way an enquiry had been conducted.

Supervisors as investigators

Confidence in immediate colleagues is important where investigations involve, as in the majority of cases in this study, small numbers of officers. It means that tight-knit groups of two, three or four detectives are the most common investigative formation. Reliance upon colleagues has been identified in earlier studies as a prerequisite of policing.[14] But working in the same small groups in case after case also means that in practice the roles of supervisor and investigator become blurred, since the supervisor is also an investigator. Whilst in the major enquiries the officer in charge

---

[14] The emphasis on police solidarity was noted in the earliest studies of policing: see, for instance, J. Skolnick (1966). See also the discussion of "cop culture" in R. Reiner (1985).

assumed a distinct role as supervisor, we found it a recurring problem in interviews with officers in charge of other kinds of enquiries to keep them on the subject of "supervision", so great was the difficulty they experienced in disentangling the two roles. Supervision itself was viewed as so minor and routine an activity that it was looked on as an abstraction without any real operational significance. It was often unclear in the interviews we conducted whether officers were talking about supervision or about other aspects of an enquiry.

This tendency to merge the processes involved in investigation was particularly evident in relation to the interviewing of suspects. For many of the cases in this sample, the crucial stage in the investigation was the interview, and, from our knowledge of these investigations, we assessed the interview as a major component of the prosecution's case in no fewer than seventy per cent of them and as an irrelevance only in five per cent. In other words, the likelihood of prosecution depended in a substantial majority of cases upon what emerged from the interview. It would be hard to overstate the importance that officers attached to the interview, and many officers saw it as their key role as supervisor actually to conduct it. No fewer than 58 per cent of the interviews covered in the study involved the supervisor as one of the interviewers. This hardly ever happened where the officer concerned was of inspector or more senior rank, but it was very common practice with supervisors of sergeant or constable rank.

Where the officer in charge of an enquiry did not conduct the interview, however, it was still comparatively rare for them to play a supervisory role as far as the interviews were concerned. This is another striking example of supervisors' reluctance to encroach upon another officer's responsibilities. This tendency was noted even in the major investigations led by senior officers. In those cases, officers might have been marginally more inclined to offer advice to interviewers than in smaller investigations, but the "hands off" policy generally prevailed.

The West Midlands stations had been equipped at the time of this study with an "audio loop" facility to enable an officer outside an interview room to watch the questioning of a suspect on a TV monitor and to communicate directly with the interviewers through an ear-piece. Although this facility was used in only a few of the cases included in this sample, it was apparent from our interviews that it tended to produce disruption and distraction for the interviewers more often than guidance. Senior officers were nonetheless strongly attracted to the idea of sitting in front of a television screen, or, better still, a bank of screens, simultaneously directing a series of interviews. But this kind of orchestration never happened in any of the cases included in this study. The reality is rather that, unless supervisors conduct the interview themselves, they only infrequently instruct officers (or even advise them) about how they should approach it.

Nor were supervisors for the most part concerned to monitor progress in an interview beyond asking officers after the event whether anything of value had emerged. This is strange since such monitoring would be unobtrusive and simple to achieve since all the interviews were on tape – in this sample on video tape – and easily accessible.[15] Had the officers in question taken the trouble to play the tapes, they would surely have noted that many of the interviews were poorly conducted – more often, it must be said, because of ineptitude than because an unduly forceful approach was adopted. There is a strong case – we would say an indisputable case – for much greater involvement of supervisors at this stage.[16] A range of problems was fairly easily identified as a result of observing the video tapes of interviews with suspects in these cases, many of which were perpetuated simply because no one had assumed a broader responsibility for ensuring that things were done in a professional manner.

The presence of a supervisor at an interview seemed to have little bearing upon whether it was done well or badly. As noted earlier, almost forty per cent of the interviews examined in the present study were assessed as having been conducted unsatisfactorily. It should be emphasised that these were not minor flaws which a pernickety academic critic might pick up; they were often fundamental. On many occasions, officers were evidently ill-prepared, conducted interviews that were laboured and repetitive, or else adopted sloppy or unfair interviewing practices.[17] In addition, things went seriously wrong with the video equipment itself in no fewer than 45 per cent of the cases included in this sample, and there were many examples of cameras malfunctioning, poor sound and picture quality, and suspects off camera.[18]

It is important, therefore, to ask how it was that the supervisory officer had not seen such things and immediately remedied them. It is unlikely that such flaws could have continued if anything like a systematic check had been made by supervisors at the stations in question. If supervisors had been unable to monitor an interview as it was actually

---

[15] In three of the four stations, a viewing room was available to enable interviews to be monitored while they were actually taking place.
[16] Home Office Circular 21/1992, issued in February 1992, placed great weight upon the importance of supervisory officers listening to the tapes of interviews.
[17] In one in six of the interviews covered by this study, for example, the caution delivered at the beginning of the interview was so garbled as to be devoid of all meaning: on other problems identified with police interviewing, see further J. Baldwin (1992) at pp. 12–13.
[18] These problems, which were more evident at the two stations in the West Midlands than elsewhere, are discussed in some detail in J. Baldwin (1991).

being conducted – and three of the four stations allowed even that facility – then it was not asking too much that they ensure at a later stage that proper procedures had been followed in the interview and that it had been satisfactorily recorded. The curious resistance of supervising officers to involving themselves in the work of others was evident in this as in other respects, and this resistance was exemplified in the following quote from an inspector in Redditch who had supervised one of the most serious and complex cases included in the sample:

> "I'm hard pressed to remember an occasion when I felt it necessary to listen to a tape. Certainly I don't examine the tapes as a matter of course. I don't see any need for that. If there are problems, then they soon show themselves and you can address that problem as it arises. I don't see it as part of my job to start random-sampling tapes to see how my officers are doing their job. If you're doing your job properly, you should have a good idea as to how they're performing anyway."

It is, then, unusual for a supervisor who has not conducted an interview to play the tapes, let alone take action based upon them. In one of the largest enquiries in the sample, the tapes of an interview were played, and it was clear to the Detective Chief Inspector who was in charge that one interviewer in a team was performing badly and that a change was required. Yet even in those circumstances, the senior officer, who was not renowned for his gentleness of spirit, recognised that it was an awkward situation to change interviewers at that stage. As he put it to us, "You're telling a detective that you don't like what he's doing and want someone else in there." His decision to change interviewer led to a certain acrimony. As he explained:

> "I said, 'I don't think he gets on with you very well,' and he said, 'We aren't in a popularity contest, gaffer.' But I've got to say you get more flies with honey than you do with vinegar. I've supervised [this officer] since and, from time to time, he lets me know that he didn't like being switched. It's very difficult. But that's what a supervisor is for, isn't it? It's no point being in a viewing room and seeing what's going on and not doing anything."

The feature of this case that makes it almost unique in the sample is that a supervisor took the trouble to watch the interview and was prepared to act decisively upon what he saw. In the vast majority of cases, the supervisor does not bother to play the tape at all.

More active supervision of interviews by senior officers would throw up difficulties, however, and efforts in that direction would doubtless meet with stiff resistance on the ground. This is because the officers who do the interviews are on the whole reluctant to accept unsolicited advice, whether it be from a senior officer, a peer or anyone else. The expectation that officers of whatever rank are entitled to respect and autonomy when carrying out their specialised role – an important precept in police culture – applies particularly strongly in relation to interviews with suspects. Indeed, it is a common view amongst the junior officers who do the bulk of interviews that senior officers, having acquired their own interviewing experience in the pre-P.A.C.E. era, are too remote from the fray to be in any position to instruct them in interview techniques. This attitude is not without justification, and it was on occasion accepted by some of the senior officers to whom we spoke. Antipathy to outside interference is deeply ingrained in police culture and is evident in the following quotes, all of which are taken from interviews with officers of detective constable rank:

Case 1 (Birmingham) "Seeking guidance about an interview is a difficult topic. It's very hard when you're interviewing. Basically someone is going either to admit or deny doing something and it's down to yourself really. I think there's a lot of pride with interviewing, and you don't like to admit defeat and admit that you couldn't do this or couldn't do that, and have to go and ask somebody. I don't think there's a lot that a senior officer could tell you about an interview. I've never gone and asked what I should do. I've always looked at it and thought that I'd go about it the way that I think is best."

Case 7 (Birmingham) "I'd welcome any guidance if it was constructive but, to be perfectly frank and honest, I don't know how many senior officers have experience of interviewing on tape or have done any courses."

Case 25 (Wolverhampton) "We work under the minimum of supervision. We're all our own bosses really. And the majority of senior officers view us as being professional enough to go to them for advice rather than doing it the other way round. I wouldn't welcome greater input from senior officers. I like it the way it is. I'm not saying that we're élitist, but C.I.D. officers with years of experience have a job to do and we've got to be able to get on and do it. Otherwise we shouldn't be in this job. The majority of the bosses have more of an administrative role. We get on with the interviews and we can't be running to the boss every five minutes."

Case 34 (Redditch) "It's automatically assumed that if rank is involved, then officers have experience and ability. But experience and ability and rank don't go hand in hand. Consequently just because someone has a lot of rank, it doesn't mean to say they've got the ability. The higher the rank, the less people are involved in interviews and investigations. They've often lost track of what is required. Many of them are not familiar with the taped interview procedure. If you listen to their interviews, they breach P.A.C.E. I wouldn't like to think that, at the end of the day, any of your conclusions from this study actually say that senior officers should be ultimately responsible for conducting interviews, because that simply wouldn't work."

Case 39 (London) "You see, I'd say that I'm probably a better interrogator than a detective superintendent is, basically because I've been doing it longer than he has. It's not the rank of the officer that's in charge of the case that's important, because the higher up you go in the police, the more administrative you become. I mean it's very rare that you'll see D.I.s from this office actually going out and crashing doors."

This expectation of officers, even of junior rank, that they should be allowed to conduct interviews in the way they think fit extends to the whole of the investigation. It tended to be the detective constables we interviewed who most vehemently defended their autonomy. Their strong view was that, if they were thought fit to head an enquiry, then they should not have to tolerate any interference from senior officers. This attitude is widely acknowledged and respected within the force, and senior officers in consequence tend to operate what they call an "open-door" policy, allowing junior officers to see them with their problems at any stage as the need arises. While senior officers often claim to cast a supervisory eye over the detective constables who are responsible for leading enquiries so that they can intervene if any problems arise, this is in truth a nominal and indirect form of supervision. It precludes the possibility of pre-empting errors or misjudgment, and indeed the prevailing view seems to be, as one senior officer expressed it to us somewhat alarmingly, "You've got to give them the freedom to make mistakes – that's the only way they learn."

The "open-door" policy is in our judgment no effective substitute for active supervision. Detective constables rarely take advantage of the arrangement, not least because they fear that it may be misinterpreted and be seen as a poor reflection upon their abilities as investigators.[19] Furthermore, given the heavy responsibilities placed upon senior management within the police service, it is unlikely that such officers will be familiar with the progress of the many investigations that are taking place in their departments. As an inspector in Redditch conceded, "There are about fifty live enquiries in the C.I.D. at the moment, but there are only ten that I know anything really about."

---

[19] As one senior officer put it:
"There is a reluctance to show a lack of knowledge in certain areas. They don't want to be seen to be lacking."

Sources of officers' confidence and expertise

Given the delegation of responsibilities to officers of junior rank, even in relation to the sort of serious cases included in this study, great trust is of necessity placed in the competence of the individuals responsible for leading enquiries. We encountered few supervisors who were critical of the way that officers had carried out an investigation, and no fewer than 95 per cent of them expressed satisfaction about the outcome of the enquiries included in this study.

We sought to find out about the training that officers had received in supervising enquiries of this kind, and it quickly became apparent that the confidence with which officers of all ranks approached investigations stemmed to a much greater extent from the experience they had acquired from doing the job than from any formal training in investigative techniques they had received. It is odd to note that the more junior the rank of supervisors, the less likely they were to have received formal training in the conduct and supervision of enquiries. A much more didactic approach is taken in the training of senior officers, and, as officers climb the police hierarchy, a determined effort is made to convert them into managers. By the time they reach the rank of inspector, many will have received substantial training in the planning of operations. For the top investigators there is now a manual, or *aide memoire* as it is called, produced by the Association of Chief Police Officers which gives a series of "reference pointers" to assist those of superintendent rank and above during the early stages of an investigation.[20] Nothing comparable seems to have been prepared for the junior officers who assume responsibility for leading enquiries.

Indeed, junior officers receive very little training at all in how to conduct, lead and supervise an enquiry. We were told, in interview after interview, how they had learned about these matters exclusively through the experience of working on similar investigations, whether with more experienced officers or on their own. It is by their actual involvement in enquiries that most officers acquire expertise, watching the way that more experienced colleagues handle an investigation. There were a number of cases in the sample which involved fledgling detectives who were being taught the methods and procedures adopted in enquiries by working alongside more seasoned detectives. Officers constantly referred to the importance of their "practical experience" which they contrasted, often pejoratively, with what they termed "theoretical" training.

---

[20] A.C.P.O. Crime Committee Working Group's "Major Crime Investigation: Aide Memoire to Initial Actions" (Home Office Scientific Research and Development Branch, 1988).

In reality, practical experience is often a hit-and-miss commodity with officers trusting to luck that their mentors are reliable models to emulate. It is, as many conceded to us, a process of trial and error, and there are obvious dangers in officers acquiring their investigative techniques in this manner. It may serve, for example, to perpetuate bad practice, and there is no guarantee that officers will learn by their mistakes, as many of them claim to do. While the question of the procedures to be followed in investigating serious criminal cases is a wide-ranging subject and one that would be difficult to incorporate into a coherent training course, there is nonetheless a strong case for arguing that much more should be done to provide officers with the basic skills that will be required in directing and supervising enquiries.[21] Experience is clearly important, but it should not be the sole method by which an officer learns how to lead an enquiry.

It is fair to observe, however, that most of the officers to whom we spoke were untroubled by such concerns, and, as noted above, they entertained few doubts about their own abilities in this regard. The success of investigations into serious cases tended to be viewed by supervisors in straightforward and pragmatic terms, recognisable to anyone familiar with popular police culture. Investigations are seen as successful if major problems have been avoided rather than because individuals have shown outstanding qualities in the course of the investigation. This laconic attitude is symptomatic of the nonchalant confidence noted earlier in this report and is apparent in the following quotes:

Case 4 (Birmingham) "It did go well. There weren't too many problems and we got a good result at the end of the day."

Case 8 (Birmingham) "I was satisfied, very much so. We had no complaints from any members of the public or anything. It was one of those operations where not a great deal went wrong."

Case 23 (Wolverhampton) "He was done. The ends justified the means. Yes, it was all done quite satisfactorily."

Case 36 (Redditch) "I was satisfied with the way the case was conducted because I basically got to the bottom of it. I was really pleased

---

[21] An Assistant Chief Constable in the West Midlands who had read this passage made the point that there is a junior C.I.D. course which includes training on how to conduct an enquiry as a major objective. He wrote:
"All Detective Constables attend this course... Detective officers value and remember the training experience they have had more than the theoretical training but the theoretical training was nonetheless there. Officers who have recently had it might be clearer about its value." (Personal communication, March 1992).

that I was able to get to the bottom of it and that the real offenders were eventually brought to book."

As long as no serious problems arise in the course of an investigation, someone is apprehended, and the court processing of those against whom a prosecution is launched is regarded as satisfactory, then most supervisors express themselves content with the outcome. It is usually only in the major operations that a more detailed and a more critical assessment is made of the way an investigation has been conducted, and this difference in approach is illustrated in the following quotes from interviews conducted with two supervisory officers – both Detective Chief Inspectors – who were in charge of large-scale enquiries:

Case 10 (Birmingham) "I was disappointed that we never got any forensic evidence. Also the difficulty with any murder enquiry is that there are a lot of things that you need to do, and you send people away to do them and they subsequently report back to you. One question was asked at that time related to the clothing the girl was wearing and some misleading information was given to us about that at the time. We later cleared up the matter, but we learnt a lesson from that enquiry. We recognised the need to backtrack on what has actually been done in the early stages. It often means that, to be sure, we have to duplicate things. I suppose, if I was unhappy, I was unhappy about that part of the enquiry and the fact that it took so long to establish what she was wearing. This misled us in the interviews that were conducted with the suspect. It's inevitable that some mistakes will be made in an enquiry like that, and I think, as a manager, that you have to accept that human beings will make mistakes. You have to be fairly tolerant. However, we have to learn from the mistakes that have been made in the past."

Case 15 (Birmingham) "We had a planned strategy all the way through. The major problem I had as regards supervision was that, once the arrest had been made, the surveillance team needed to debrief and prepare their notes and I had an arrest team on standby ready to deal with the interview. Now it's very difficult with surveillance to collate all the intelligence that you've gathered that day. It takes two to three hours to prepare the notes. So we'd got people who'd been arrested and we needed time to be able to gather the evidence together from outside before we actually started the interviewing. But in general it was a good job, everything went well."

This difference of approach according to the scale of the operation is reflected in the way that supervisors convey their feelings about the investigation to other officers. So nominal is the supervision in most cases that many officers found it odd that we should ask about whether they conveyed their feelings of satisfaction (or otherwise) to others involved in the investigation. In only five cases in the sample did a supervisor formally do this, and, in the remainder, they tended to take the view that it would be both presumptious and unnecessary for them to express any view about the investigation in more than an informal manner, if indeed they bothered to do so at all. The idea of conducting a lengthy *post-mortem* on cases that have been concluded is not highly regarded within the police service, and, as the following quotes indicate, supervisors by and large avoided the kind of backslapping that we as outsiders had tended to think would be commonplace.

Case 6 (Birmingham) "There would be a lot of chatting about it, either before, during or after, when you sit down at the end of the day, have a cup of coffee and a smoke and think, 'Well, we sorted that one out.'"

Case 7 (Birmingham) "I don't think that you say that a job has been brilliantly done or start patting each other on the back when you've charged somebody, because you always know that you've still got to get them through the Crown Court. I don't consider it to be a job well done until I can go up to the victim and see a smile on their face when I tell them what's happened in court."

Case 15 (Birmingham) "When you have a good job, we gather together and have a little debrief. In fact I think it was in the bar on a Saturday night and we had a jar about it. To be honest, if you're on a job like that, you don't need anybody to tell you if it's going well. It's a bit like football, like scoring goals, if you like. If it's going well, you're full of it. If you're down, you don't need to be told because you know it isn't going as well as you wanted it to."

Case 23 (Wolverhampton) "Recognising that we've done well very, very rarely happens. Recognising work done badly happens all the time. We seem to deal in negative qualities rather than positive things. You don't know when you're doing things well except by the absence of comment!"

Case 30 (Redditch) "You have to understand the police culture to understand how we talk to each other. It's not a question of taking a bloke to one side and saying, 'You did a good job there, pal,' because they wouldn't want that. They know they're there to do a job. Policemen are fairly practical creatures and they would become very cynical if you started giving them big 'attaboys' on the back."

Case 42 (London) "When you work together as a team, you wouldn't have to tell them that you were satisfied with the outcome. They know because it's something that you're always discussing."

Case 45 (London) "I can't remember saying, 'Well done.' We wouldn't talk like that anyway. It's not the way I would work. We would be more likely to have a laugh or a joke about it afterwards."

It is clear, then, that many of the supervisors to whom we spoke regarded questions relating to the congratulation and encouragement of colleagues as curious notions. By contrast, the enquiries supervised by officers of the rank of inspector and above were much more likely to involve a detailed assessment of progress – "briefings" and "debriefings" as they are known in the vernacular – and formal acknowledgement of the contribution made by individuals. In that sense, the style of supervision adopted by officers of senior rank was much more managerial in emphasis, with correspondingly greater weight placed upon briefing sessions and other forms of reinforcement for the officers involved in an investigation.

Conclusion

Two distinct models of supervision emerge from this analysis of the investigative process. Major enquiries led by senior officers are supervised in the sense that the officer in charge of the investigation directs operations and assumes a full managerial role in the enquiry. By contrast, in investigations involving small numbers of officers, the ethos of teamwork prevails. The formal supervisor is usually no more than a name on the case papers. The dichotomy is such that it could almost be said that in the former case investigations are supervised, whilst in the latter they are not.

Our abiding impression is that too great a responsibility is being placed on the shoulders of junior officers. The cases included in this study were very serious in nature, and, as a detective constable in Birmingham observed of a section 18 assault case we had been discussing, "If you try to equate the weight or value of that particular job with something in industry, you wouldn't have someone on such a low echelon in a company dealing with that thing because it would be too big a responsibility." The question that is raised in this research is therefore whether it is appropriate for officers of constable rank to be expected to investigate and supervise offences of this gravity.

We have noted that the detective constables we interviewed were confident about their own abilities to cope with running such investigations, but it is revealing that three quarters of them voiced reservations about the laxity of supervision in serious investigations within the police service as a whole. Almost all officers to whom we spoke could easily recount horror stories of working with others whose supervision was not highly regarded, and there are of course enough well-publicised instances of miscarriages of justice to indicate that there has been on occasions in the past a total breakdown in standards of supervision.

It is interesting that the criticisms of standards of supervision that were made by the officers we interviewed were not directed at immediate colleagues but instead at senior officers. The latter were often seen as being out of touch from the hurly-burly of investigations and so in a weak position to comment upon the way they were being conducted, still less to supervise them. However, it is likely that such attitudes reveal more about the prevailing police culture (a basic tenet of which is that officers have confidence in their immediate colleagues) than about how well these officers might have conducted enquiries.

The expression of such views is also indicative of the nature of supervision itself. Other than in the small number of military-style operations in the sample, supervision was superficial or non-existent, and it depended too heavily on small tight-knit groups of officers of detective constable rank operating as self-contained and largely autonomous entities with little direct supervision from above. While this may be an efficient and effective unit for most purposes, its performance is ultimately dependent on the competence and integrity of the individuals concerned. And if officers are incompetent, dishonest or even corrupt, the mechanisms of supervision currently in place provide little effective check on their activities. The "cop culture" makes for strong and cohesive groupings, and, as long as things run smoothly to all outward appearances, the organisation itself is relatively powerless when it comes to controlling and supervising their activities.

There is no easy solution to this problem, although there is no doubt in our minds that it must be tackled primarily within the police service itself. Some thought needs to be given to the existing rank structure and, as far as the many routine investigations with which we have been concerned in this report are concerned, it seems to us that improvements in standards of supervision might best be effected through an enhancement of the role of sergeant. At present the rank of sergeant within the police service tends to be viewed as an incremental promotion from the rank of constable, and, while they are formally senior to constables, this formality belies an everyday reality where, particularly in the C.I.D., sergeants tend often to be treated as equals by junior colleagues.

The sergeant is, then, very much the *primus inter pares* within the C.I.D., and there are powerful structural imperatives within the police service which produce the relative impotence of the rank. Two factors in particular are significant in this context. First, the difference in pay between constables and sergeants is not great (not nearly as substantial as between sergeants and inspectors, for example), and this affects the way that sergeants are viewed and how in turn they view themselves. Second, and more important, the daily realities of police work tend to prevent sergeants from distancing themselves from their colleagues. The workload of the C.I.D. as a rule ensures that sergeants are required to become as immersed in the investigation of offences as detective constables.[22] As one inspector put it in interview, "Detective sergeants become little more than detective constables because it's a question of all shoulders to the wheel." In such circumstances, sergeants' authority and capacity to supervise are greatly reduced.

Making the rank of sergeant more substantial would provide a viable alternative to the present "open-door" policy of senior officers to which we have already referred. The sergeant is in a much better position than officers of higher rank to be acquainted with the strengths and shortcomings of investigating officers and is also better placed to find out about any problems which may develop during the course of an enquiry carried out by a junior officer. By increasing the sergeant's authority and opportunities for supervision, effective intervention in the routine enquiry would be greatly facilitated. Needless to say, increasing the responsibility and authority of the sergeant rank would have resource implications. It would entail enhanced training and remuneration, and would therefore be costly to implement.

There is, however, more to be gained from seeking to improve standards of supervision within the police service by bolstering existing arrangements than by imposing structural change from outside. One attraction in giving greater substance to the rank of sergeant is that it would provide a mechanism to raise standards of supervision that could easily be introduced. Furthermore, it would not require unduly cumbersome procedures which might well be resented by police investigators and be undesirable on other grounds as well.

Seeking to strengthen supervision at ground level by this means seems to us more likely to be effective than alternatives based upon interposing, as has often been suggested, a senior prosecutorial or quasi-judicial figure at the head of major enquiries. The involvement of outside figures in criminal investigations is a feature of certain inquisitorial systems, but such notions fit uneasily within the adversarial processes which have traditionally operated in this country. Such proposals do nonetheless enjoy a certain appeal as mechanisms for countering what are seen by many as unhealthy police tendencies to pursue single-mindedly

---

[22] The Assistant Chief Constable in the West Midlands (*ibid*) made the following observation in this connection:
"The difficulty [with increasing the supervisory content of the sergeant's role] has always been that they spend most of their time investigating. With the present workload, it is hard to see how that can change."

the conviction of suspects.[23] The problem of police officers becoming psychologically committed to a certain line of enquiry and unwilling to test alternative theories has been recognised in this country for many years, and, when we put to the officers we interviewed the idea that some outside official might be involved in major investigations, we were surprised that it was favourably received by many of them. Some officers had no strong opinion on the subject but it is interesting to note that, of the remainder, as many favoured the idea as resisted it.

Yet further questioning revealed that this attitude was not based on any genuine enthusiasm for having Crown Prosecutors or other officials actively involved as the supervisors of investigations (for which there was no support), but was rather a recognition that access to immediate legal advice on an enquiry could be a useful by-product. It was only if outsiders could be employed as adjuncts to an investigation – as the servants rather than as the leaders – that officers appeared to be sympathetically disposed to their appointment.

Notwithstanding this somewhat cynical stance, there seems to us to be no strong argument in favour of diluting the investigative function of the police, and little to be gained by attempting to turn Crown Prosecutors into supervisory officers, let alone making them directors of operations.[24] As a detective in Redditch expressed the point to us:

> "I think it would be better to try to improve the existing machinery rather than scrapping what we already have. If you've got a piece of machinery and you've got a supervisor watching it, it's no good changing the supervisor if the machine isn't working properly. You can change him a dozen times and you won't get the machine to work any better."

Although there would seem to be little advantage in having Crown Prosecutors as supervisors of enquiries, considerable benefit might nonetheless be derived from seeking to involve them early on in the investigative process. Crown Prosecutors already participate at an early

---

[23] These tendencies are discussed, for example, by P. Devlin (1979) at pp 70–76; M. McConville and J. Baldwin (1981) at pp 96–98, and M. McConville, A. Sanders and R. Leng (1991) at pp. 200–202.

[24] A similar conclusion has been reached in one of the Royal Commission's studies. In an enquiry (conducted quite separately from the present study) into criminal procedure in France and Germany, Leigh and Zedner (1992) write:
> We believe ... that some part of the public clamour for the introduction of an examining magistrate represents an attempt to solve, by means of a magic wand, problems which can only be resolved by restructuring of the existing system and by the expenditure of time and money in the administration of criminal justice. (p. 68).

stage in some enquiries,[25] and there is in our view much to be gained from extending this practice. One main benefit is that they could examine whatever evidence the police have collected at that stage and more effectively direct that further enquiries be made along lines they deemed appropriate.[26] Earlier involvement of the Crown Prosecution Service would serve in this way to enhance confidence in the integrity of investigations. If all materials collected by the police in the course of an investigation were handed over to Crown Prosecutors, then they would be in a much stronger position than at present to provide some real direction to enquiries.[27]

Although criticisms have been made in this report about aspects of the police investigations we have examined, it is appropriate that we convey the admirable qualities that were evident to us when we spoke to the officers concerned – their enthusiasm, *esprit de corps*, commitment, sense of fair play, loyalty and the like. We did not conclude that these were officers who were thrusting remorselessly for conviction; nor did we find that they were often uncaring or slipshod about the way that the people with whom they dealt were treated. But the conclusion we draw, after having spoken at some length with these officers, is that the procedures that presently operate, as far as the supervision of investigations is concerned, contain the potential for laxity, if not abuse. They allow too great a latitude to officers of constable rank in the way that they conduct enquiries, while at the same time imposing heavy responsibilities upon them. As we have noted in this report, supervision is often regarded by officers as an abstract and artificial concept, almost as a figment of the academic imagination. It is time that the idea of supervision, based upon real responsibility and authority and grounded on rank, was resurrected.

---

[25] One Crown Prosecutor observed:
"We do try to encourage the police when they are investigating a serious allegation to, in fact, contact us at a very early stage so that we can discuss the case and try and assist them with any evidential or other problems that we may foresee in the investigation of a particular case." (Personal communication, March 1992).
It was clear, however, from the comments made to us by representatives of the Crown Prosecution Service, that such involvement on the part of Crown Prosecutors is infrequent and unsystematic.

[26] This would also allow the Crown Prosecution Service to determine the sensitive question of what material should then be disclosed to the defence, and it would seem to make better sense to allow Crown Prosecutors to decide this matter than to leave the decision with the police.

[27] Even in relation to minor matters, there are strong arguments for allowing the Crown Prosecution Service instead of the police to determine, in the light of the available evidence, when a caution should be administered. Given the great number of cases involved, this would, however, be a costly procedure to implement.

References

Argyle, M. (1988). *Bodily Communication*. London: Methuen.

Baldwin, J. (1985). 'The police and tape recorders'. *Criminal Law Review*, pp. 695–704.

Baldwin, J. (1986). 'The tape recording of police interviews with suspects'. In Deakin, N. (ed.) *Policy Change in Government*. London: Royal Institute of Public Administration.

Baldwin, J. (1991). 'Videotaping in police stations'. *New Law Journal*, 141, pp. 1512–1516.

Baldwin, J. (1992). *Video Taping Police Interviews with Suspects – an Evaluation*. London: Home Office Police Department.

Baldwin, J. and Bedward, J. (1991). 'Summarising tape recordings of police interviews'. *Criminal Law Review*, pp. 671–679.

Baldwin, J. and McConville, M. (1979). 'Police interrogation and the right to see a solicitor'. *Criminal Law Review*, pp. 145–152.

Bottomley, A.K. and Coleman, C. (1976). 'Criminal Statistics: The police role in the discovery and detection of crime'. *International Journal of Criminology and Penology*, 4, pp. 33–58.

Bottomley, K., Coleman, C., Dixon, D., Gill, M. and Wall, D. (1990). 'Safeguarding the rights of suspects in police custody'. *Policing and Society*, 1, pp. 115–140.

Bottomley, K., Coleman, C., Dixon, D., Gill, M. and Wall, D. (1991). 'The detention of suspects in police custody'. *British Journal of Criminology*, 31, pp. 347–364.

Brown, D. (1989). *Detention at the Police Station under the Police and Criminal Evidence Act 1984*. Home Office Research Study 104. London: HMSO.

Devlin, P. (1979). *The Judge*. Oxford: Oxford University Press.

Dixon, D. (1991). 'Politics, research and symbolism in criminal justice'. *Anglo-American Law Review*, 20, pp. 27–50.

Easton, S.M. (1991) *The Right to Silence*. Aldershot: Avebury.

Greenawalt, K. (1974). 'Perspectives on the right to silence'. In Hood, R. (ed.) *Crime, Criminology and Public Policy*. London: Heinemann.

Greenwood, P.W., Chaiken, J.M. and Petersilia, J. (1977). *The Criminal Investigation Process*. Lexington: D.C. Heath.

Home Office (1989). *Report of the Working Group on the Right of Silence.* London: Home Office.

Irving, B.L. and McKenzie, I.K. (1989). *Police Interrogation: The Effects of the Police and Criminal Evidence Act 1984.* London: Police Foundation.

Kaye, T. (1991). *"Unsafe and Unsatisfactory"?* London: Civil Liberties Trust.

The Law Society. (1988). *Advising a Suspect in the Police Station: Guidelines for Solicitors* (2nd Edition). London: The Law Society.

Leigh, L.H. and Zedner, L. (1992). *A Report on the Administration of Criminal Justice in the Pre-Trial Phase in France and Germany.* Royal Commission on Criminal Justice Research Study 1. London: HMSO.

Leng, R. (1992, forthcoming). *The Right to Silence in Police Interrogation: A Study of Some of the Issues Underlying the Debate.* Royal Commission on Criminal Justice Research Study. London: HMSO.

McConville, M. (1992). 'Videotaping interrogations: police behaviour on and off camera'. *Criminal Law Review*, pp. 532–548.

McConville, M. and Baldwin, J. (1981). *Courts, Prosecution, and Conviction.* Oxford: Clarendon Press.

McConville, M., Sanders, A. and Leng, R. (1991). *The Case for the Prosecution.* London: Routledge.

McKenzie, J. (1990). 'Silence in Hampshire'. *New Law Journal*, 140, p. 696.

Mawby, R. (1979). *Policing the City.* Farnborough: Saxon House.

Moston, S., Stephenson, G.M. and Williamson, T.M. (1990). 'Police Interrogation Styles and Suspect Behaviour: Summary Report to the Police Requirements Support Unit'. Institute of Social and Applied Psychology, University of Kent.

Ramsay, M. (1987). *The Effectiveness of the Forensic Science Service.* Home Office Research Study 92. London : HMSO.

Reiner, R. (1985). *The Politics of the Police.* London: Wheatsheaf.

Reiss, A.J. (1971). *The Police and the Public.* New Haven: Yale University Press.

Reuss-Ianni, E. and Ianni, F.A.J. (1963). 'Street cops and management cops: the two cultures of policing'. In Punch, M. (ed.) *Control in the Police Organization.* Cambridge, Mass: MIT Press.

Royal Commission on Criminal Procedure (1981). *Report.* Cmnd 8092. London: HMSO.

Sanders, A., Bridges, L., Mulvaney, A. and Crozier, G. (1989). *Advice and Assistance at Police Stations.* London: Lord Chancellor's Department.

Silberman, C.E. (1978). *Criminal Violence, Criminal Justice.* New York: Random House.

Skolnick, J. (1966). *Justice Without Trial.* New York: Wiley.

Steer, D. (1980). *Uncovering Crime: The Police Role.* Royal Commission on Criminal Procedure Research Study 7. London: HMSO.

Wolchover, D. and Heaton-Armstrong, A. (1991). 'The questioning code revamped'. *Criminal Law Review*, pp. 232–251.

Wright, D. (1986). 'Silence at the police station'. *Law Society's Gazette*, 83, pp. 269–271.

Zander, M. (1972). 'Access to a solicitor in the police station'. *Criminal Law Review*, pp. 342–350.

Zander, M. (1979). 'The investigation of crime: a study of cases tried at the Old Bailey'. *Criminal Law Review*, pp. 203–219.